1997 SWARTHMORE LECTURE

D0315422

Previous Convictions

and
end-of-the-millennium
Quakerism

CHRISTINE TREVETT

QUAKER HOME SERVICE

First published in 1997 by
QUAKER HOME SERVICE,
Friends House,
Euston Road,
London NW1 2BJ

ISBN 0-85245-290-X

cover & layout design by David Goddard

Printed in Wales by Cambrian Printers
Aberystwyth Ceredigion SY23 3TN

Preface

THE SWARTHMORE LECTURESHIP WAS established by the Woodbrooke Extension Committee at a meeting on the 9th December 1907: the minute of the Committee provided for an 'annual lecture on some subject relating to the message and work of the Society of Friends'. The name 'Swarthmore' was chosen in memory of the home of George and Margaret Fox, which was always open to the earnest seeker after Truth, and from which loving words of sympathy and substantial material help were sent to fellow workers.

The lectureship has a twofold purpose: first, to interpret to the members of the Religious Society of Friends their message and mission; secondly, to bring before the public the spirit, the aims and fundamental principles of Friends. The lecturers alone are responsible for any opinions expressed.

The lectureship provides both for the publication of a book and for the delivery of a lecture, the latter usually at the time of assembly of the Yearly Meeting of the Religious Society of Friends (Quakers) in Britain. A lecture related to the present book was delivered at the University of Wales, Aberystwyth on the evening of 4th August, during the 1997 Yearly Meeting of the Religious Society of Friends in Britain.

Foreword

REVIOUS CONVICTIONS HAS BEEN hard to write. In
preparation for it I discovered lots of examples of
the kind of confusion I had come to feel and when I
read research done about our Society (and some of that
figures in this book) I recognised myself and everyone
else in it. But at the same time I wished that more Friends
were willing to face squarely the kinds of questions which
such research findings posed.

This book is in two parts - 'Confession and Confusion',
which tells you something about where the writer is
coming from, and then - 'Faith, Values and their
Transmission'. Readers who dislike endnotes and
bibliographical references may stick to the text without
losing much, I hope. I have included quite a lot of such
references, nevertheless, to draw attention to the kinds of
discussion which are going on in and around the Society.

My thanks go to the Swarthmore Lecture Committee
and to Elisabeth Salisbury and Ruth Heine, in particular,
for their encouragement and help. As usual the staff of
the Library at Friends House were invaluable. Joan and
John Southern gave me access to material pre-publication
and I learnt much from visits to informal 'special interest'
groups, of which modern Quakerism has many. I was also
welcomed to Canaan Monthly Meeting of the Friends in
Christ (Plain Quakers). In addition I had useful
conversations about subjects discussed in this book with
Paul Ballard, Joel Edwards, Muhammad Akram Khan-
Cheema, Daniel Levy, Elaina Rothman and Maggie Roux.

Mary Ann Ebert worked on the mauscript and David Goddard saw to its publication, I am indebted to them. A special diolch is owed to Hugh Matthews and Gwilym ap Robert.

Finally I thank some of the young Friends of Bridgend, Pen y Bont ar Ogwr, who have allowed me to make use of their writing. I promised I would name them...

... so 'THANK YOU' to:

Andrew Dimond
Catrin Harries
Dafydd Harries
Mark Dimond
Matthew Davies
Meirion Harries
Nathan Trevett
Philip Davies

Rejoice in the presence of children and young people in your meeting and recognise the gifts they bring... How do you share your deepest beliefs with them?

Advices and Queries §19

Llawenhewch ym mhresenoldeb plant a phobl ifanc yn eich cwrdd, gan gydnabod y doniau sydd ganddynt... Pa fodd yr ydych yn cydrannu'ch daliadau dyfnaf â hwy?

Cynghorion a Holiadau §19

Contents

Previous Convictions

PART ONE

confession
and
confusion

chapter one

OPENINGS

THIS IS THE BOOK of the 90th Swarthmore Lecture to be given, marking the 1997 Yearly Meeting of the Religious Society of Friends, held in Aberystwyth.

It is little more than two years to the end of the millennium and throughout the 1990's the Society in Britain has been engaged in self-analysis. There has been belt-tightening, some reorganisation and some fearful prognostications. There has also been hopefulness, with much hard work and decision-making. There has even been optimism.

Quakers are known for their optimism - I imagine it is something to do with having a dissenting view about original sin. Our Friend the late Gerald Priestland, broadcaster about religion par excellence, wrote in his autobiography that their optimism was one of the things that drew him towards Friends.[1] In 1995, on the other hand, another religious broadcaster, based in Wales, confessed to me that what most irritated him about Quakers ('lovely people') was 'their relentless optimism'. Either way we are known for it.

The Religious Society of Friends has seen great change and altered circumstances in recent decades. Even familiar names are altered. No longer (since 1995) do we speak of London Yearly Meeting but now of Britain Yearly Meeting. And the Meeting for Friends in Wales, which did not exist at all before the decade of the '90s, had already by 1996 not only survived but decided to change its name subtly and meaningfully, to Meeting of Friends in Wales.

On the surface Quaker life carries on much as usual - there are still Yearly Meetings and Swarthmore Lectures and in those two things Friends are continuing to be what they have always been: listeners, ardent chroniclers of their own histories and their own activities, and analysts of those activities. At the same time there continue to be people in our Meetings who remain totally unaware that anything at all has been happening, while some of the heart-searching and changes which are well known to other Friends may indicate that we are not immune to the psychological impact of millennialism. As the year 2000 approaches we too may suffer from, or be touched by, the feelings and fears which go with the changing of aeons.

Certainly we have begun to see in our Meetings, and in some of those groups who use our Meeting Houses, the marks of that New Ageism which is an upsurge of searching in novel ways for a spiritual dimension in life. And like a rite of passage, such as coming of age, marriage or the death of parents, the approaching millennium's end reminds us that we are still here, and that things are no longer the same. This anniversary of the birth of Christianity's founder (give or take a few years for chronological uncertainty in the records) finds Christianity different from its beginnings. It finds our relation as Quakers to Christianity uncertain, tenuous, even for some one of hostility, in a way and to an extent which even Quakerism's most ardent seventeenth century critics could not have imagined. Quaker Christianity has always been 'different'.

What can we say before You?

The time, I suggest, leaves us not wholly certain who and what we are. We are confronted with questions about our own identity. Who are we? What were we? How are we? Where are we? Where are we going? - and most important of all, perhaps, Why are we? - like the child in a lift who posed his mother the stunning question 'Mummy, what is that man for?' Previous Convictions does not claim to answer such questions, but I do not doubt that the Society should be searching corporately for the answers. To some extent it has begun to do so. The process will not be painless.

I am told that there is a Friend who has the following plain-spoken message on his answer-phone:

> Who are you and what do you want? Most people spend a lifetime answering those questions. You have forty seconds.

He should first have given his own phone number, of course. The question 'where are we?' is very important, and it is also important to know where the questioner is coming from. In the chapters which follow in Part One (Confession and Confusion) it will be clearer where I am coming from.

'Where are you?' is an important question for the Religious Society of Friends as it approaches the millennium. It is the first question in the Bible, put to Adam, and would never have needed to be put if Adam were not, according to the myth, now estranged from God and trying to avoid God. All else follows in Christian theology from that first question 'Where are you?'

'Although British Quakers may be clear individually as to their stage along a spiritual path', wrote Keith Redfern at the start of his essay in the book Searching the Depths: Essays in Being a Quaker Today, 'as a religious community it seems that we are still seeking unity on our overall spiritual position.'[2] The words community and unity are important in Previous Convictions.

Are we personally or corporately at one with God or losing sight of God? Are we, individually or corporately, trying to avoid this 'God' business altogether, refusing even to use the word? Are we ceasing to think 'corporately' at all? Are we creating metaphorical fig leaves to disguise the fact that we have been stripped of much that we had in the past and in this age of 'isms' are still not sure whose clothes we should be wearing?

The question 'where are we?' also links into other questions. 'Where were we before' or (to put it differently) 'where have we come from?' It moves inevitably to 'where are we going?' My own mind moves to the Siddur [3] of Judaism, curt and challenging:

What are We?
What is our life?
What is our love?
What is our justice?
What is our success?
What is our endurance?
What is our power?
Lord our God and God of our ancestors
What can we say before You?

A long memory

It is 340 years since, in 1657, George Fox travelled through Wales in the aftermath of the James Nayler affair,[4] sometimes with John ap John for company, who had been the first Quaker convincement from Wales,[5] and sometimes with Thomas Holme, the weaver from Kendal who was a Quaker apostle to Wales. Fox was a man of long memory. Years later he recorded in his Journal that at Aberystwyth he discovered the ostler at the inn stuffing his own pockets with the oats which his thrifty self had paid for. His openings, of course, had convinced him of the reality of the 'ocean of darkness', as well as of the ocean of light. For some in Wales the Light had not yet triumphed. It is 350 years since, in 1647, a spiritually struggling George Fox began to experience such 'openings'. They brought him encounter with the Christ who could speak to his condition and who taught his people himself, without need of intermediary:

> Now after I had received that opening from the Lord that to be bred at Oxford or Cambridge was not sufficient to fit a man to be a minister of Christ, I regarded the priests less... As I had forsaken all the priests, so I left the separate preachers also... And when all my hopes in them and in all men were gone, so that I had nothing outwardly to help me, nor could tell what to do, then, oh then, I heard a voice which said 'There is one, even Christ Jesus, that can speak to thy condition'.[6]

Three hundred and fifty years is a short span of time compared with the double millennium which is soon to be commemorated. The early Friends claimed, nevertheless, to represent 'primitive Christianity revived' and as late as 1925 W R Inge ('the gloomy dean' but friend of Woodbrooke and of Rendel Harris[7]), was writing thus in The Platonic Tradition in English Religious Thought that

> The Quakers, who of all Christian bodies have remained nearest to the teaching and example of Christ, are the smallest of all denominations... [emphasis mine].[8]

There are Friends who would claim as much today. But there are many Friends, and more than will ever have been the case throughout the Society's history, who would regard the issue of whether the Society is Christian as an irrelevance. Here has been one dilemma for this writer of Previous Convictions as she has come up against questions of who, what and why we are. Let me share some more with you, by way of introduction.

15

Writing this book

Previous Convictions has been very hard to write.[9] The task put to me initially was to address the matter of the transmission of faith and values in Quakerism today. The process of writing at first became akin to devising Advices and Queries for myself - except that the Queries mounted and I was floundering about Advices. I thought to subtitle it Confessions of a Confused Quaker. In time the confession and confusion became an integral part of the book.

As in the Siddur, the Queries we use as Quakers are discomforting. But afflicting the comfortable as well as comforting the afflicted is part of the role of religion and of religious people. The Advices and Queries ask questions about how and what we learn, and how we put the knowledge into practice. They are not meant to be easy. I once complained to Harry Crann, clerk of Meeting of Friends in Wales, that it was something of a chore being the Quaker representative on Cytûn's[10] clergy-dominated - and clergy-training obsessed - Forum for Theological Education in Wales. He responded 'Tell them, we are not without education. We are the only denomination to set regular exam papers. What else are the Queries?'

And one Sunday, with university examinations on my mind and an inadequate grasp of Welsh in my head, I invited a Friend in my Meeting (where we read the Advices and Queries bilingually) to read from the Arholiadau (examinations) instead of the Holiadau (Queries). It was not inappropriate.

Fortunately we do not report in public how often, individually and corporately, we pass! As for me, there were plenty of queries, but little by way of advice was emerging as I thought about Previous Convictions.

Foundering and floundering

For months I wrote nothing. The questions multiplied. Some of them were theological, but I did not want to write a book about theology. Some were about what happened to religious movements, sects and denominations over time, about authority, institutionalism and change and decay. But I am not a sociologist of religion. I am a historian of religion, but this could not be simply an historical analysis.

Neither theology nor history could be ignored, I decided, and for that matter, the sociologists of religion had things to say to us. But still my attempts to integrate all these things in my mind with the task of addressing faith, values and their transmission were not going very well. I was foundering on the rock of modern Quaker diversity.

I began to despair. I could decide to be simply descriptive (this is where we seem to be, for good or ill); I could opt for being blatantly prescriptive ('faith'? 'values'? this is it, these are the ones - we should get on with it!); I could be restrictive (such as considering only Friends' work in the Adult Learning sphere, and throughout our history). But no - none of these seemed right. Instead I became very conscious of my own confusion. What was this thing called Quakerism anyway? Was it possible to know any longer? And were there other Friends 'out there' who were equally confused and ill-at-ease?

I suspected that there were. I suspected, too, that there were other Friends who were less than fully aware of the reality of pre-new millennium Quakerism, though evidence was plentiful. So after much floundering, I decided that this could not be a book of answers. I did not have any. I came to suspect, too, that it would be a writing rather unlike many previous Swarthmore lectures.

This was to be no 'academic' study of Quakerism. If it emerged as confused, it would be because this Friend is confused and she dares to think that the Religious Society of Friends is too. Certainly I do make use of some things which academics have written about present-day Quakerism - notably sociologists. But much of the language of this book is the language of personal experience and of anecdote.

As I worked on it, some parts began to look like autobiography. That is not accidental. At a time when Quakerism embraces a greater diversity of adherents than ever before, it is important for readers to know at what point on the broad spectrum of Quakerism a writer is to be placed. It is appropriate, too, because in Part Two of Previous Convictions such personal spilling of beans, in trust, is advocated. It is part of our responsibility to teach and to guide.

Soon after having accepted the invitation to be Swarthmore lecturer I almost contacted the Lecture committee and asked to be released. That was because I had read the introduction to Martin Davie's study of Quakerism and theology,[11] in which he stated that the Swarthmore Lectures represent a useful measure of the thinking of Quakers at any one time. I had no expectation that I would be speaking for Quakerism or that I would be representative of what Friends en masse in Britain Yearly Meeting in 1997 were thinking. But I stayed with it, because I had been asked and I had said yes.

The title 'Previous Convictions'

Why the title Previous Convictions? It isn't without problems. In a year in which the Swarthmore Lecture is delivered in Wales, it is a pun which won't translate into Welsh. I like puns and ambiguous titles. They give me visions of sleepy librarians shelving Well Dressing alongside books on couture, or (a title I found in Friends House Library - all concerned with the author will forgive me) Batter My Heart next to More Delicious Things To

Do with Offal. This Previous Convictions would not sit well in Criminology. But the conviction word, and its shifts of meaning, were important to me.

The Religious Society of Friends, like the wider Christian Church, the society we live in, and many other things, is the product of all it has been. It is not created ex nihilo in each generation. It bears within itself the record of its shortcomings and its wrongs, as well as of what, God willing, it has been and done in true discipleship. It has to learn from its past and in some respects free itself from the shadow of its failings, its 'previous convictions'. That is the negative connotation of the title.

Convict/convince is also a 'weighty' Quaker word. For the first Friends of Truth, in the seventeenth century, conviction was convincement; i.e. they experienced proof certain of the truth of that message and of the Messenger, which was brought to them. Truth carried conviction. They were, moreover, changed and reformed people because of it. So they were convicted/convinced in the sense also of being conscious of past failure. The ocean of darkness in themselves and the world had been pointed out more starkly by the power of the Light they experienced and now walked in.

Guilt, in Christian (especially the apostle Paul's) understanding, is not a psychological state of ill-ease, that is merely 'feeling guilty'. Guilt is a forensic reality, meaning that in relation to God, who is in a position to judge, the person is guilty. Humankind is not God, is not even, in most respects, Godlike. The first Friends of Truth, no less than other Christians, faced the reality of having previously been 'in the wrong', they had not been right with God. Some had been at war even with themselves. But their convincement was joyful, for they were certain (convinced) that they were no longer convicts in God's eyes. The Light (of Christ) was love and life and truth and power. They were liberated, Spirit-empowered people, in the vanguard of change for a world which was in transformation.

This use of the word conviction I have placed alongside previous, to show that past knowledge, experience and its working out in practice will be important for what I write. I am interested in the history of religion, Christian, Jewish and not least Quaker. But such things are a backcloth for looking at the present and the future too, as well as the impact of our own religious histories on what we believe and do. They are a backcloth for asking questions about core values, core beliefs, about whether we have them and how, whether, we transmit them to others.

Threads through the book

What will you find in Previous Convictions? I expect that you will find some things you recognise and others you cannot identify with. You will not necessarily find things descriptive of your Meeting, though on the other hand it may be you, or me, that I am talking about at times. If you are a regular reader of The Friend and are also familiar with the kinds of discussions which go on in Friends' conferences, Quaker Journals, recently published books about and by Quakers, then probably much of this will not be new to you.

You will find running through Previous Convictions some threads which have woven themselves into my own life. There will be (A) my response to 'coming home' in Quakerism, together with my own pre-Quaker 'previous convictions' and my subsequent fear of throwing out babies with bath-water. Then (B) the questions I listed in preceding paragraphs were 'we' questions ('who are we?' 'where are we going?'), and that is significant. Issues of identity, belonging and the group will be woven through this writing too. I too have to ask myself what makes me (or makes me not) part of the 'we'. I asked a friend who is a Rabbi of the Reform Jewish tradition how she judged the success of her transmission of knowledge, of values and of a sense of identity when preparing someone for conversion to Judaism. There is a point, she said, at which they start saying 'We...'

This leads me to a confession of sorts (and confessions are part of this book). I have been associated with the Religious Society of Friends for only seventeen years, and a member for sixteen. I do not think that that is very long. People who see Saul of Tarsus (St Paul) as 'the man who ruined Christianity' mutter 'there's nothing worse than a convert'. Those who are wary of the zealotism of some in-comers in propagating a language and identity which was not originally their own (and modern Wales knows all about that) wonder about grandmothers and sucking eggs. Gerald Priestland's autobiography told of how, having become a member,

> I went bouncing round the Society, talking my head off and urging Friends to pep up their theology and decide what they really believed in.[12]

I recognise the temptation. On the other hand, at the end of the twentieth century, so many of us are in-comers to the Religious Society of Friends. The majority of us were not born into it,[13] and that is not without its problems. There is as great a danger, then (and Wales knows all about this too), that incomers will seek not to change themselves one iota but rather to 'be themselves' in a congenial setting and seek to conform the aboriginals to their understanding and way of doing things.

Now I come to (c). Something else which will keep raising its head in Previous Convictions is my long-standing affection and respect for Judaism. You may have noticed this already, after just a few pages. It has been bolstered by friendships, by teaching about it and by

21

sharing Hebrew, its language of Scripture, prayer and liturgy, with hundreds of students over the years. There are so many memorable sayings, sharp insights, pithy quotes and, of course, jokes in Jewish writing, both sacred and otherwise. And its mode of wrestling with God has spoken clearly to my condition at times. But for all that I learn from it, my 'we' is not the 'we' of Jewishness. And for me that is significant too.

In a year when the Swarthmore Lecture is being delivered in Aberystwyth (D) becomes notable. It is my consciousness of being Welsh.

The status of the Welsh language in London (now Britain) Yearly Meeting came to the fore in the Yearly Meeting of 1994 and in the preparation of the revised Book of Discipline. Here too was a matter relating to identity and the 'we' of being a Quaker. It raised questions about the validity of differences (in this case of language) among us, and the capacity of such differences to threaten or enhance our sense of unity. Hundreds in Wales who listened to George Fox in 1657 had understood scarcely a word he said, but were moved by that Spirit in which he too spoke and now (with translations included) the resulting revised Book of Discipline, known as Quaker Faith and Practice (1995), has items in Welsh. Increasingly, too, the pages of The Friend acknowledge the existence of Friends in Britain Yearly Meeting for which Welsh is the language of the Scriptures and the language of their dreaming.

Nevertheless the questioning about the language had set me thinking about the other ways in which the evident differences between Friends, and the religious language they use, are sources of discomfort to others among us. It caused me to ask what words do we use and (metaphorically speaking) in what language do we communicate, to those who are as yet outside of Quakerism.

So these are the kinds of things which will keep surfacing throughout Previous Convictions, though none to an overriding degree, I hope. Finally in this chapter...

An aside

I tend to go in for asides... actually Hebrew, the language of Judaism and of half of the Christian Bible, and Welsh, the language of some of our Friends in Wales, have certain things in common.

> The Welsh language lays claim to high antiquity, as being a branch of the Jaspian, or that dialect of Hebrew spoken by the posterity of Japheth

wrote John Evans in his Letters During a Tour Through North Wales in the Year 1798 and Other Times, published in 1804. In the Victorian age and the early twentieth century the occasional eccentric tried to show that the affinities were enough to develop theories of Britain as home to lost tribes of Israel! The likenesses are superficial.[14] Nor do Friends any longer hasten to learn Hebrew (as a few did in the seventeenth century). In the millennial kingdom (which was imminent, they thought) surely Hebrew would be the language spoken. That was the language of God himself as shown by the Bible, the language of the Eden-Paradise state and presumably it had been the language of all humankind before its hubris and the events of Babel turned the world into a place of babble, of shattered communication.[15] Here is a whole set of previous convictions which has disappeared from Quaker thinking, at least since the advent of the present century, the impact of modern critical biblical scholarship and the Manchester Conference.[16]

So far as the language of communication with God is concerned, the Welsh never experienced doubts. In the land of Wales it was taken for granted, and expressed as passionate certainty (at least to the English) that in heaven the angels speak Welsh. It tells you something about this Quaker writer that she (unlike some Friends, she knows) does not rule passionate certainty out of court. It is good to know that what you have is of lasting worth, approved by God, and deserving of transmission. Passion and certainty - 'conviction' - however, seem to me to be on the wane in some quarters of the Religious Society of Friends.[17] And for some Friends, I know, the very idea of welcoming and promoting such conviction will cause them to read no further.

chapter two
THE OPENER

In the name of Allah (God), the Merciful, the
Compassionate.
Praise belongs to God, the Lord of all Being,
the All-Merciful, the All Compassionate, the
Master of the day of doom.
Thee only do we serve; to Thee alone we pray for
succour,
Guide us in the straight path,
the path of those whom Thou has blessed,
not of those against whom Thou art wrathful,
nor of those who are astray. [1]

THESE WORDS ARE the opening words of the Qur'ān
(from the chapter Al Fatihah, or 'The Opener').
They are as meaningful to Christians and Jews as
they are to Muslims. The three religions share a heritage
of poetic, prophetic teaching which likens the spiritual
journey to a path to be followed, and which also reckons
on there being that Light which enlightens the way.[2] It
is a view of the religious life which presupposes a goal.
It is possible to go astray and to fail to reach it, but the
path leads to Something, Somewhere, understood, if
only partially. There is a conviction in this, an
expectation that those on the journey know in what
state they hope to end up.

This chapter of Previous Convictions, and the next
ones, are about my own dilemma. The verse above
expresses certainties and requests with which the first
Friends of Truth would readily have associated
themselves. But today, it must be said, many in the

Religious Society of Friends could not associate themselves with any such certainty, whether that of the Prophet-mediated Qur'ān or of our forefather George Fox. In other respects, too, we have changed.

What is unique about religious communities, Muslim, Quaker or whatever, is that they worship. The what of Quaker worship is now less clear than it used to be, at least it is less clearly defined. The fact is that some Friends would not wish even to think in terms of worship, just as they would not speak of goals or destinations. Increasingly I hear the view that the journey is enough, indeed all. Having expectation about the where and the why of our travelling, and claiming to know anything very much about the way or the process of enlightenment, is to commit the sin of neo-orthodoxy. 'Sin' is not a word in use, however. As one respondent notes in Ben Pink Dandelion's sociological study of Quaker theology,[3] perhaps 'more Friends now turn to Matthew Fox than George Fox', preferring (to echo the title of Matthew Fox's book on 'creation spirituality') Original Blessing to ideas of sin.

All this is a far cry from the echo of the prophet Jeremiah (6:16) which was printed on the monthly issue of The British Friend from 1846 onwards: 'stand ye in the ways, and see, and ask for the old paths, where is the good way, and walk therein'. But that was a time of battle for the soul of Quakerism (not the first, and not the last such battle), and that verse, about standing at crossroads and looking, was part of the ammunition.

Part of my dilemma is that I have come to realise the extent to which I do not share a vocabulary of faith and values with some Friends in the Religious Society of Friends. Let me illustrate. Let me return, first, to Al Fatihah.

'What Canst Thou Say?'

An observant Muslim who read the opening words of the chapter might know at once that I am not one too. The fact of having the sayings of the Qur'ān in translation, and without Arabic parallel text or apology, is a clue. Islam knew, long before it became a truism for students of languages or semiotics, that 'all translation is interpretation'. So for much of its history Islam has discouraged the translation of its holy Book.

The words are not just words, after all, says the Muslim. For while the Qur'ān presents itself as the final message to humankind, it also presents itself as the message made in the Arabic language.[4] Islam has retained the original language, though interpretations of its meaning change. For Muslims the Qur'ān is not about something, such as the history of late Byzantine and Persian imperial tensions, or a commentary on the development of monotheism in Arabia or even a fine example of poetic prophecy or a biography of the Prophet, Muhammad. It is not about something, it is something. It is revelation.

This may be all very interesting, but it assumes a view of past revelation and of Scripture which Quakerism has never shared. In any case it brings its own problems.[5] The 'what canst thou say?' of Quakerism demands more than reading knowledge of a text, in any language (so too does Islam, of course). Nevertheless the business of revelation, ongoing, was important to Quakers too.

When George Fox first uttered the question that is well known to many Friends, it surely presupposed that what Christ and the Scriptures had said was indeed already known, even if it was not internalised and enlivened and interpreted by the Spirit:

> You will say Christ saith this, and the Apostles say this; but what canst thou say? Art thou a child of Light and hast walked in the Light, and what thou speakest, is it inwardly from God?[6]

We stand now on different ground. In the 1990's Quakers as a group can no longer assume such knowledge as a point of departure for a greater demand. The 'words' of traditional religious belief may not in fact be known to some Friends (this is discussed in Part Two of Previous Convictions). Some have rejected them, described them as irrelevant or indicative of an inferior insight, an outmoded tribalistic understanding: such statements stand in the letters pages of The Friend with regularity. Moreover 'the Light' as many Friends now choose to understand it is divorced utterly from reference to the Christ, and 'that of God' in each has become an ill-defined truism.[7]

Early Friends had also made challenging use of Scripture (they were engaged in what those who study early Christian prophecy and teaching would call 'charismatic exegesis'[8]), reinterpreting it, taking what Jesus and the Apostles had said and making of it a rallying cry for justice, a warning of retribution and about reaping the whirlwind, a demand to be heard (not least by women[9]). As the year 2,000 approaches, these things are of no concern to many of us. Some of us, indeed, think that what we were matters not one jot. All that matters is what we become. Such things tell me that in many respects I differ greatly from some Friends in the Society.

Like a way of life, a religion is constituted not just by what we do but by the framework within which we understand what we do. For me, Fox's words about the Christ, the Scriptures and 'What canst thou say?' had meaning against my background of taking seriously 'traditional' Christian religion (though not necessarily of being wholly comfortable with it - see chapter four). Some time in the late 1960's I had been stopped in my tracks one day in a library, on turning accidentally to the dedication page of a book by the leading New Testament scholar W D Davies. Normally I skip over such pages but I had found there a quotation from the bard Gwenallt (the poet D Gwenallt Jones, 1899 - 1963), in Welsh, which is Davies's mother language, though it is not mine.

There is a difference, Gwenallt was saying, between knowing the words and knowing the Word which informs them (... wybod y geiriau heb adnabod y Gair), though Welsh puts it better. Like French which has savoir and connaître; or the German use of wissen and kennen, the Welsh gwybod doesn't express the intimacy of knowing which the verb adnabod does. English has lost this personal, intimate sense of even the single word 'know' (though people still speak with a wink of 'know in the Biblical sense' cf Genesis 4:1). Years later when I read about George Fox, I thought of Gwenallt. In many respects the Quaker path that I took was a familiar one.

In writing Previous Convictions I have had to ask myself where, in the 1990's, is the assumed starting point for our coming to Quakerism? What is it in newcomers' intimate knowledge and understanding which is being transformed? Indeed is transformation (which I take for granted as a function of religion) something which is of no interest to many Friends, who prefer rather to 'be themselves' and to learn to love their essential rightness and goodness? (a view I have heard frequently among Quakers). And given that we should not take it for granted that any transformation will be, as in George Fox's time, a transformation within an assumed framework of language, belief and experience which is Christian then what does Quakerism look for instead?

Such questions loomed large in my mind, given that I was supposed to be writing about the transmission of faith and values. They loomed larger when I read the sociological study of Quakers which was done by Caroline Plüss.

Her research found that Quakers are not, in fact, very interested in discovering whether the would-be-member of the Religious Society of Friends understands what it is about. Friends' failure to outline what is expected of a member indicates, she says, (and contrary to what one might think on other grounds) 'that Quakers are apparently not a sectarian group' at all.[10] This seemed to me to raise troubling questions nevertheless. One of them was whether we were failing to help others understand what Quakerism is because we no longer knew ourselves.

All Things Partial and Provisional

I came to wonder whether Quakerism of recent decades (by which, in this case, one has to mean individual Monthly Meetings) has been asking of those who seek membership whether the very concept of transformation - 'convincement' - is meaningful to them at all? Have we been questioning the correlation of seeking to finding and asking after the 'from what? to what? and by what?' of the enquirer's experience? Or has the fact of enquiring become enough, so far as many Friends are concerned?

As I pondered the matter of writing about transmission of faith, I found myself asking more urgently whether Quakerism knew what it was. How were those of us who were in it to determine whether the seeker was finding, or whether the road to finding was recognisably a Quaker one? Or were such questions now without meaning?

Dared we any longer speak of well-trodden paths and of assured guidance for those who are open to it?

Were some Meetings refusing to offer signposts, even declaring that they were redundant? These were not new questions in my mind, though having to write Previous Convictions had brought them into focus.

* * *

At a gathering for elders at Yearly Meeting in Exeter, 1986, one Friend asserted that she always refused to answer attenders' or enquirers' questions, on the grounds that there was nothing she could say which would not be partial or provisional. I did not find the matter of partiality or provisionality surprising. It comes of us not being God. But there was such general assent in that group, about not wishing to say anything, that I became troubled. If George Fox were to return to confront us, would the answer to 'What canst thou say?', I wondered, be not only 'not very much'[11] but also 'and that's fine with us'? Were we in danger of losing our ministry of teaching, and to our peril? And in a time of uncertainty and change, wasn't teaching just what 'the world' was in need of?

Carrying on regardless

I had come to realise some time ago that my own too-ready assumptions about what was a 'given' in Quakerism were very wrong indeed, and that I had been carrying on regardless of a different reality. For example, in August 1995 Quaker Home Service and Woodbrooke published in the Quaker Resources for Learning series some substantial study documents. This was under the title Who We Are: Questions of Quaker Identity.[12] I had written the portion which considered early Friends' theology and the early Christian church, and, as is usually the case, there was to be a series of questions at the end.

My first question was phrased in a way which suggested that 'convincement' was a path which brought a person to the point of membership. The question went on about what brought convincement, and convincement of what? Evidently I was thinking (and assuming that everyone else was thinking) that convincement was the desired outcome of the process of transmission of faith and values in Quaker circles. The editor thought otherwise - with more wisdom about the Society than I had. Friends should be asked whether they agreed that 'convincement' was indeed significant.

Then there was the moment in December of that year when I discovered - by accident and from reading the findings of one of my graduate students in feminist theology - that a British Meeting House and its garden had been used for the Lammas rites of an all-female neo-pagan group. Altar, ritual casting of a circle, displaying of natural objects and incantations figured in the proceedings.

I was not surprised to discover that the Meeting concerned had not been aware of what use was made of its premises. But I was stunned (yes, that's the right word) and bewildered to discover some Friends who seemed pleasantly excited at the prospect. There were Quakers who declared 'it all sounds rather nice' and who, I imagined, would find it difficult to countenance circumstances (meetings of the Territorial Army apart, perhaps) under which Quaker premises should not be used. I found others, of course, who thought differently.

Such things have brought home to me the gulf between my Quaker self and some of the other Friends with which I share the Society in its diversity. The gulf may not always be apparent - and the capacity for Friends' worship (and especially the silences and the unsaid things in it!) to bridge differences and release mutual love and tolerance is not to be underestimated or undervalued. But we should not pretend that it does not exist or that difficulties may not be simmering unacknowledged because of it. Some of the difficulties impinge on the transmission of faith and values.

Significant Polarisations

These things made Previous Convictions hard to write. Whose faith were we talking about transmitting? What values? Of course the Society was well aware of its own diversity. In her sociological study of modern British Quakerism Caroline Plüss had examined one source of potential difficulty. This is the one which tends to come to most Friends' minds and it was an

> ongoing belief controversy, labelled by some Friends as a disruptive conflictual situation risking the division of the Quaker movement.[13]

She took as her extremities in the Quaker (theological) diversity the New Foundation Fellowship and the Quaker Universalist Group. I am not certain that this is the most significant polarisation in the Society, however, and in Previous Convictions I suggest that we should be looking just as much to the differences among Friends which are based on loyalty to, and dismissal of, the tradition and testimonies of the Society; and commitment to, or dismissal of, Quakerism's understanding of how the will of God is discerned. These differences, I think, will not necessarily correlate with sympathy for the New Foundation Fellowship or the Quaker Universalist Group - and most Friends belong formally in neither one of these, in any case. They are important differences.

'In all things permit liberty, act in charity, strive for unity'

Readers of The Friend of some time past will wonder whether I have erred in a well-known quotation which from 1861 appeared on its cover (but does no longer). This was the aphorism 'In essentials unity, in non essentials liberty, in all things charity'. What I have actually quoted is an alternative version proposed by Kathleen M Slack in her 1967 Swarthmore Lecture:

> Who cares greatly about liberty in non-essentials.
> It is precisely in the things regarded as essentials
> that liberty is most desired. Likewise it is in them
> that it is most difficult to achieve unity.[14]

The alternative aphorism seemed more fitted to the reality.

Kathleen Slack was by profession a sociologist. Her overview of constancy and change in the Society had led her to conclude that in its three hundred years (writing in 1967) it had swung between extremes and then 'come to rest in freedom not authority', in normality (not in the peculiar), in tolerance (not assertion of discipline), in variety rather than conformity.[15]

Freedom, tolerance and variety: these were Kathleen Slack's key words. Writing thirty years later, however, I have to ask myself whether the philosophy of 'in all things permit liberty' now has triumphed in the Society to the detriment of a search for unity and for a corporate witness on matters of the day.[16] Others, I know, believe that Quaker diversity is not just bridgeable but it is creative of something no less recognisably Quaker than that which arose from the Society's previous convictions. Present-day Friends are divided on such matters. We try to keep quiet about it, but we are. Sometimes we can not keep quiet, and the tensions break forth, as at Yearly Meeting in 1994, giving rise to the editorial in The Friend which followed:

> We lived our Quakerism ... it was not always a pretty sight ... hurt and insensitivity were blatantly exposed as we heard yet did not hear each others' experience ... ugliness ... mockery, unspoken but visible ... belittling ... Anger, straightforward and raw ... some went home grieving ... This Yearly Meeting has changed my understanding of Quaker life.

The fact of diversity

What is agreed is that diversity is a marked feature of the Religious Society of Friends and Quaker writers often present this in markedly positive tones. Caroline Plüss, an 'outsider', in questioning Friends about beliefs and receiving a variety of non-definitions, open-ended definitions, specific definitions and experiential definitions, concluded that there was 'a high degree of diversity ... Quaker belief may be defined as individualistic',[17] or 'open-ended', as Ben Pink Dandelion put it in his own sociological study of Friends. There exists a 'neo-orthodox pluralism' (the pluralism itself being part of the orthodoxy), and a Quaker 'double culture', according to Ben Pink Dandelion. This is of a liberal belief system and a conservative organisational structure. Even his finding that belief in 'that of God in each' was a unifying factor among Friends (though there was no necessary agreement on what it meant) was contradicted by Caroline Plüss's findings.[18]

Does any of this matter? Does it matter that the 'creed of pluralism' involves a shift from 'optional nonconformity within the group to culturally prescribed nonconformity representative of the group' (?)[19] Is it indeed the case that 'A commitment to religious truth' must mean a willingness to ... be prepared to have in common that we have nothing in common' (?).

I think that probably it does matter. And I am less sanguine about the prospect of having nothing in common than many Friends seem to be. I wonder where such a philosophy will lead us as a Society - as the 'we' of Quakerism - rather than as a loose-knit collection of individuals. Ben Pink Dandelion wrote that 'behind the shared jokes and the attempts at inclusive language lie deeper divides', though they are 'often invisible in the silence'.[20] Not all silence is good.

* * *

The matter at issue, Ben Pink Dandelion wrote, is that ancient Quaker term Truth. A distinction needs to be made, he suggested, between

> a pluralism additional to a single God, or Truth, and a pluralism of Truth. The perceptions of the non-credal belief system, as a system which permits universal licence in terms of belief, indicates that there is a potential threat to the singularity of Truth.[21]

This, I think, is the measured language of academic caution. The idea that Truth is redundant, and that truth is a matter of personal preference, or individual leading only, is already a recurring motif in late twentieth century Friends' circles - or so it seems to me. This being so, what then should be the faith and values which we transmit, beyond those which sanction the diversity and individualism which now are facts? How do we discern what we are to DO, and as a Society?

Opening ... a can of worms

Quite a number of Friends have been writing in ways which show that there is an awareness of rapid change in the Society over recent decades. And they have written with thought for the possible implications of such change - for patterns of membership in the Society, for active participation, for our social testimony or for beliefs. Even The Quaker Song Book [22] preserves reference to one kind of change, which is not unlike my own response to contentment with the provisional and partial.

Pleasaunce Holtom's song 'The Doubting Quakers' was written some years ago. Here are some of the verses:

Doubt has become a Quaker virtue
So open-ended, we're blown by every wind,
Not admitting we're less than we might be
Let alone that we've sinned,
We're all in search of God,
We're good at silent seeking,
Seekers for ever, finders never,
But silence can be a drug,
When we ought to be speaking.

Tolerant to a fault, pleading perplexity
Glad there are lots of things we can discard.
Finding undoubtedly means commitment,
So we don't seek too hard ...

Sociological research uses more circumscribed language. 'The content of Quaker belief is open-ended', Plüss wrote, echoing Ben Pink Dandelion.[23] As for 'blown by every wind', I wonder whether that might not prove to be another way of saying that

Quaker belief is highly flexible in absorbing cultural change, or changes in the ideological orientations of the membership.[24]

Whatever language we use, it seems that if the seventeenth century saw the muscular, 'weighty' Friend who took on all-comers in the cause of Truth (or at least those are the ones which the historians celebrate), and who saw the shift from Seeker to finder, than the late twentieth century is bringing to the fore the feathery Friend, standing light in relation to certainty, and not averse to succumbing to the ever-shifting winds of fashion and of change. Of course the wind/spirit (for the same word serves for both in the Hebrew as in the Greek) does blow where it wills (John 3:8). This is a fact to which both kinds of Friends, centuries apart, might decide to appeal in defence.

* * *

So The Opener, taken from the Qur'ān, was just a starting point for this chapter, to draw attention to some of its themes. The Opener speaks of certainty, faithful reliance on a God who is known and trusted, paths, and the possibility of a straight one at that. It speaks also of those who are on paths which are undesirable.

This is not the language of late twentieth century Quakerism. It is not the language of compromise or agnosticism; it is not the language of relativism or political correctness. It has nothing to do with 'terminal tolerance'. It could be matched, of course, in many other writings 'which reveal the ways of God' (as the Advices say).[25] Certainly it is not comfortable or even always comforting language and it gives no truck to ideas that the human being is anything other than subject to God, albeit to One who is in all things compassionate, a provider of paths but not morally blind-eyed or liberally absent-minded. There is right and wrong to be distinguished, it is saying, and the inspired prophet and teacher function to discern and distinguish. There are paths which are best avoided and guides who lead us up spiritual cul-de-sacs, in this kind of religiosity at least.

Starting from Al Fatihah, then, what this chapter may be opening is a can of worms. Faced as I am with the task of writing about faith, values and their transmission, I confess that I am concerned about rainbow Quakerism, relativism and individualism; about the possible development of a culture of tolerance and 'caring', of a 'therapeutic community' which is to the exclusion of tackling and unravelling the difficult ethical and theological knots. I weary of Friends pleading that 'all things are partial and provisional' and I am wary of almost all truths being negotiable and of 'selling out' to some unattractive aspects of modernity, including a cult of uncertainty.

But what about the Red Book?

In the view of some Friends the answer to all such questions or dilemmas has been provided through the revision of the Book of Discipline - 'it's all in the red book'. I remain unconvinced even though I am very glad we have such an anthology. I meet people of diverse Christian traditions who know of it and ask where they can get a copy, regretting that their own tradition has nothing similar.

After the publication of Quaker Faith and Practice in 1995 (which is The Red Book) John Lampen reviewed it in The Friends' Quarterly.[26] He knew it had been created with great honesty, effort and love. But he isolated as weaknesses some of the very things which I had in mind too, in a book which must serve as theology, anthology and source of inspiration.

There was the matter of 'the present book's grasp of our history' and its 'overemphasis on the voices of today' (with most of the many 20th century quotations coming from the last thirty years). The most 'up to date' quickly becomes dated, he observed, and being less informed about our Christian origins than we used to be, we may also be losing contact with our own history. Though I know very well that Quakers like to stress present experience,[27] I had had similar questions in mind. Quaker Faith and Practice, with its multitude of quotations, does indicate that the Society is not averse to citing experience from the past, but this was not used sufficiently to inform us on things which were being presented as if they were dilemmas peculiarly of our age, when in fact they were not. The working out of previous convictions was ignored due to emphasis on the recent past and the present.

And there too was the provisional and partial. Quaker Faith and Practice is a work which does not fear to present doubt and uncertainty as realities in our experience. That is surely right. Churches generally, and increasingly, are learning to talk openly of such matters. But I also identified with John Lampen when he wrote the following:

> I put a name to what I was missing; words of power. The book lacks the certainties of our forebears and in places has an oddly tentative feel [Emphasis mine].

Would an enquirer, he wondered, want to probe the force of those mays ('Are they more than a maybe?') in the Advices and Queries, though such tentativeness, he admitted, reflected the contemporary mood. I had wondered whether Quakerism too easily reflects, rather than challenges, the contemporary mood and so too did Jonathan Dale, in his 1996 Swarthmore Lecture Beyond the Spirit of the Age. There he expressed the fear that the dominance of

> relativistic morality and metaphysics amongst contemporary British Friends is gravely damaging to many aspects of Quakerism.

> In particular it weakens the basis for action ... Its individualism provides poor defences against

the secular world; it destroys the sense that our faith seeks to implement timeless values in a world of change.[28]

All of this, it seemed to me, was a far cry from 'The All-Merciful, the All-Compassionate, the Master of the Day of Doom. Thee only do we serve... guide us'; it is some distance from the certainty implied in Jeremiah's 'old paths' and 'good way', and compared to what George Fox and his contemporaries knew to be possible answers to the question 'What Canst Thou Say?' our own seem to be oddly tentative. Some Friends, I know, would not wish to speak either of God or of seeking God's will in a group, but would prefer the secular language of 'looking for a way forward' or 'finding something we can agree on'. That, it seems to me, is part of the problem.

Perhaps what we need are 'openings'.

chapter three

NO NEW THING
UNDER THE SUN ?

THERE ARE WRITERS who have researched with some thoroughness the present Quaker position and the path to it. Apart from the studies of Ben Pink Dandelion and Caroline Plüss, there is Martin Davie and the conclusions of Alastair Heron[1] on the basis of his research among Meetings in the North of England and elsewhere. Other studies of British Quakerism have been completed recently or are under way.[2] Swarthmore lecturers, too, have been hinting (or saying explicitly) that some developments in modern Quakerism are of a kind potentially damaging to the Religious Society of Friends and sapping of its spiritual vigour. The lectures of John Punshon (1990),[3] of Brenda Clifft Heales with Chris Cook (1992) and of Margaret Heathfield (1994) may be mentioned, as well as Jonathan Dale (1996).[4]

Swarthmore lecturers, I dare say, are expected to say such things. A congratulatory catalogue of Quaker achievements and insights would not fit the bill of a Swarthmore Lecture at all! But some may be asking whether pre-end-of-the-millennium Quakerism is one of doom and gloom? Are some present day Friends falling prey to a golden-ageism which believes that previous convictions were of necessity superior to present ones and that all was well not long since? I think not. This chapter is for burial of 'golden-ageism'.

It is not that I do not share the general tendency to optimism which was mentioned in the opening *paragraphs of Previous Convictions. I do. Change, in any case, is a must in any religious group if it is not to atrophy, and openness to its possibilities is even more of a must in a group which declares itself responsive to the Spirit. Despite the perception of the hymn-writer,[5] change can be due to regeneration or revitalisation, it can be a positive transformation. But I also believe that watchfulness is needed, for by contrast not all change is good.*

Going too far

'This sort of thing, may if not watched, sometimes go too far.' The sentiments are commonplace. The words are those of Joseph John Gurney, in a letter to Jonathan Hutchinson, written after Yearly Meeting in 1833. It was a time when many in the Society were under 'deep and painful exercise' he wrote. And why? Because of the prevalence (his word) at that time of 'somewhat different views of divine Truth'. There was (to use the language of twentieth century Quakerism) diversity of opinion. He called it divergence.

> We have thou knowest always been accustomed
> to watchmen at opposite gates

he wrote, and watchfulness was needed, lest there result a 'diverging too palpable to be welcome'. He was proved right. An unwelcome diverging (in the forms of competing English Quakerisms) emerged.[6]

When Ben Pink Dandelion used the 'gatekeeping' analogy in his 1993 thesis, it indicated something quite different from watchful oversight for moves which signalled doctrinal change.

Gatekeeping in the Quaker group, he wrote, 'is solely based on adherence to the behavioural creed, and the claimed identification of the individual with the group' (emphasis mine), while in Sociological Analysis he noted some Monthly Meetings' willingness to admit 'any applicant', adding that 'Non Christians and atheists were accepted into membership during the period of participant observation'.[7]

There are present-day Friends who fear that Quakerism is 'going too far' and is bereft of active gatekeepers (the gatekeeper/watchman is a prophetic figure, as will emerge in Part Two of Previous Convictions); that it allows unquestioningly too much claimed identification and is insufficiently rigorous for its own future good when considering applicants for membership. I am one of them. There are Friends, by contrast, who argue that no separation between members and non-members of the Society should exist (though in reality little does in any case).

More radically there are Friends who talk, more in corners than openly I think, of more major schism than that which has been associated already with the Friends in Christ of the 1990s;[8] predicting a reproduction of aspects of fragmented American Quakerism, which nowadays goes beyond Hicksite or Gurneyite or Wilburite or programmed/unprogrammed kinds of divisions, so that one analysis has spoken of the unprogrammed tradition alone in terms of ethical mystical/universalist/New Foundation/conservative/ecumenical Christian/agnostic-atheist/pagan/Aquarian-New Age and Twelve Step kinds of Friends.[9] And there are British Friends, I'm sure, who have no inkling that any such concerns exist or of what turmoils there are under some surfaces.

'Our poor degenerate ... Society'

Much of the 'change' complained of, feared for and rejoiced in nowadays has parallels with events in our Quaker history. I tend to be of the school of thought which quotes Ecclesiastes 1:9 and says 'there is no new thing under the sun'; a study of history leads some people in that direction. Humankind generally, by contrast, does tend to look back to a mythical 'golden age', usually of about twenty years or perhaps a couple of generations past. Such retrospection is usually mistaken and God forbid that there should be among Friends an anguished regret for the past which hinders our actions for the present and the future. There must be a sense of perspective, as well as a proper wariness about 'going too far'.

British Quakerism has never been without soul-searching and debate. There has always been diversity; particularly in terms of doctrine, rather than of practice. There has always been a flinching in the face of change, not least where books of discipline were concerned. There is no new thing in these respects. The 19th century saw the Fritchley separation,[10] talk of a 'poor afflicted remnant' after revision of the Book of Discipline,[11] and decades-long pained correspondence between Friends in Britain and America. In 1862, William Hodgson Jr (1804-1878) was writing from Philadelphia to Thomas Drewry about 'the nominal Society in England … the train is off the track'; while more than twenty years previously a British Friend, Anne Jones, had written from Stockport to this same Hodgson, regretting 'the lamentable state of our poor degenerate and bewildered Society … (and) those who are suffering for these innovations'.

Joseph John Gurney's name was on everyone's lips, and for his detractors it was a question of loyalty to the previous convictions of Friends. 'Either our ancient Friends were mistaken or J(oseph) J(ohn) G(urney) is unsound', Hodgson wrote in a letter to Thomas Frankland.[12]

So when I read the pained editorial in The Friend following Yearly Meeting in 1994 and the revision of the Book of Discipline, I was reminded of many an incident in the Society's past and reminded too that there was no Golden Age. That editorial had spoken of 'being unreconciled'; of seeing this place which is called 'home' invaded 'by those I cannot call friend', and 'the impossible task of living with them, slowly learning to recognise them as fellow-seekers, though speakers of another tongue'.[13]

And my mind went back to the year in which an 18th century Friend had found Yearly Meeting a pleasant experience because (unusually) it had not been invaded by Quakers from America or Ireland, solicitous for the right ordering of London Yearly Meeting Friends! The passage concerned speaks to me of an element of the sardonic which I regard as healthy and a guardian against neurotic religion. Others, I'm sure, will regret its 'tone'. The writer was Joseph Woods, London linen-draper, and the year was 1792.

> Our Yearly meeting has been conducted with much moderation and harmony. Luckily we had no Americans to tell us what the practice is in their country, and our Irish brethren seemed contented to eat of the fat of the land without murmuring. The women (I ask pardon, I mean our women Friends) sent no proposals of innovation. They told us, however, as usual, that the Lord had owned them, an expression which, being so oft-repeated, seems to imply a fear that they should find no owner.'[14]

So perceptions of change and decay in the Society, fears for its soul and about factionalism are nothing new in themselves. 'Golden-ageism' and lack of perspective are rightly to be debunked.[15]

Something different

Nevertheless Friends should think it possible that something qualitatively and quantitatively different may indeed have been happening in, and to, Quakerism of recent decades. They should think it possible that the Society's responses (and those of individual Meetings) to change may not always have been for the best and that *'this sort of thing may, if not watched, sometimes go too far.' For Quakerism, once again, is not what it was, or so Swarthmore lecturers and a growing number of others have been saying. In some respects the situation it faces is new. Here are some reasons why.*

• *The time is past when the Religious Society of Friends was self-sufficient and cushioned from 'the world'.*

• *'The world' in many respects has caught up with it. It has seen the rightness of Friends vision and now does out of respect for 'human rights' and as humanitarian aid those things which Friends initiated from radical, prophetic response to 'leading'. This is no bad thing, but (like the British losing an empire and never finding a role) Quakers are now challenged with regard to their social testimony.*

• *Its mighty moneyed Friends are no more.*

• *No longer is the majority of its members born into Quaker families, with the opportunity for 'socialisation' and the advantages of blood ties which that brought.*

• *As never before, attenders are choosing to remain attenders, not seeking membership.*[16]

• *And never before in the present century or the previous ones, I think, has there been such a time in which there seems so little that can be regarded as 'in common' amongst British Friends. The previous convictions have been spent, or newcomers have joined us without them.*

• And never before, I think, would enquirers and attenders have complained that trying to find out what Quakers believe and know and demand of those who join them (rather than what many of them do, which is clearer), is like wading through treacle.

chapter four

PREVIOUS CONVICTIONS

or

WHERE THE WRITER

IS COMING FROM

RELIGION SKIPPED A generation of my family, and it was that of my parents. My grandparents had no conventional religion either, but in their generation, other members of the family had. Thus when I began to attend the local Baptist chapel at about the age of ten, older chapel-goers could point out the faded faces of long-dead great aunts and uncles in the photographs on the vestry wall. The chapel was vast and solid. The Sunday School benches were of oak and iron. The religion was the same, and I am immensely grateful for it. I cannot remember a time when I did not have a sense of God. Certainly that sense long preceded my attendance at Baptist Sunday School.

My visits to Pentecostalist children's gatherings in earlier years were chiefly to do with being a terrible show-off. I was a determined 'performer'. They would give you an orange if you sang! Nevertheless I preferred the sonorous, the beauty of the polished chapel with its gold-fronted organ soaring above the painted wrought balustrade, and the fact that I had friends who attended there. When we sang 'Hear the pennies dropping', at the time of the collection, it was in Welsh.

The chapel, in a small South Wales mining town with many Quaker associations but no Quakers, was a place of prayer, culture, philanthropy and music. The people were kind. Many of them were well-educated, for already, in the 1950's when I started to attend, the working classes had largely deserted the chapels. There were few miners and their wives in the pews.

Instead there were more of the headteachers and teachers, the nurses, the shopkeepers, the local bank manager and (a touch of the exotic and interesting, we y bobl ifanc/the young people thought) an airline pilot who lived in a flat in the metropolis of Cardiff! He was also gay and amusing. His widowed mother, a quiet figure in the back pew, was kept in the dark about his job 'because she'd worry', while his longsuffering English partner sat through many a year of sermons in a language foreign to him. Then there was 'Will'.

Will was keeper of hymnbooks and checker of the organ locks. Will was lame, shambling and spoke little. By this time (the early 1960's) he was already a man in his sixties. He had a speech defect so marked that conversation took a lot of concentration on the listener's part. Most people in the locality regarded him as an imbecile. He was not. Gentle and literate, Will was made a deacon, attended the business meetings and, although often silent, was party to decision-making. This 'promotion' was because he was (as one adult explained to us youngsters) 'a man of faithfulness'.

'Suffer little children ...'

'The young people' in my age-group numbered about ten boys and girls. We were an inseparable group. In a mostly harmless way we were a gang, full of mischief. I was one of the two who arranged the minister's baptism suit - an all-in-one affair with boots attached - over a large yard brush and hung it from the balcony, so that in the evening gloom the unfortunate chapel cleaner encountered what she first took to be a swinging corpse. Occasionally we were pious.

I felt a pang of recognition when recently I read the autobiographical stories Fishers of Men by Gwyn Alf Williams.[1] Gwyn Alf, who died in 1995, was a professor of history at the university where I teach, and a child of Merthyr Tydfil, close to where I too was born. He will be remembered by many television viewers as the charismatic teller of historical (and not so historical) tales, while striding across mountains. His small stature and his stammer made him immediately recognisable.

Gwyn Alf had been part of a chapel gang. In the 1930's it had produced, clandestinely, Our Own Magazine, which was more than our gang did. His were harder times. The cold war apart, ours were more peaceful and less propagandist, so we had nothing akin to being a fascinated 'strictly extramural branch of the Hitler Youth' or (later) 'almost overnight an extramural branch of the Third International'. Nevertheless our days of 'gangdom' were also ones in which plans were laid, values were absorbed, serious questions were asked and rebellions began. I was baptised at sixteen, against the clear instruction of my parents. I could do no other.

On being a Baptist

When I tell Friends of my Baptist background they sometimes express sympathy, assuming an unbending rigour and a Scriptural conservatism which can be characteristic of such a denomination. But the fact is that in my teens I was first introduced to modern critical biblical scholarship in that chapel. There was opportunity for questioning discussion, though it was probably no coincidence that these things tended to occur during periods of interregnum, when the chapel had no full-time minister and the deacons and senior members ran things. My baptism was at precisely such a time.

My nine years of association with the chapel fed my passionate interest in the Bible, in particular. The chapel secretary, a classicist, would give lessons in Greek for those committed to New Testament study. But it was also a root of my anti-clericalism. I left the Baptist denomination in my mid-twenties, depressed by contact at university in England with a narrow conservatism that I had never encountered (except among some clergy) in allegedly conservative Wales. For our Friend Alison Leonard, who wrote Telling our Stories, it was the Christian Union which was her undoing.[2] For me it was BAPSOC, the university Baptist Society.

Still I have to say that it is often hard to disabuse Friends of the idea that Baptists are by nature a stumbling-block to ecumenicism, liberalism and inter-faith activity. It depends.

Spiritual Homelessness

By the time I had left the Baptists I was thoroughly embroiled in the study of religion; a research student and a school teacher of religious studies and music. I was also married to a former Roman Catholic. I had met him while both of us were on Voluntary Service Overseas. Together we were spiritually homeless.

My public act of commitment had been made at sixteen. It was made with almost no understanding of the expectations of the denomination, but in emotional response to what I understood to be the expectations of God. 'More glands than God', a cynical clergyman friend of mine observed about teenage conversions. Coming from a non-religious family, I had no idea of what members of my extended new family might have in mind. My baptism was a formative experience in my life, nevertheless. To this day I can date that anniversary more quickly than the anniversary of my marriage.

From time to time in the 1970's I dragged my husband to various places of worship in the West Yorkshire town where we now lived, to test the waters. I do not believe that religion is a solitary occupation and I was looking for companions. On one memorable occasion, during a miners' strike, a Methodist lay-preacher began castigating the greed of miners. This was too much for my husband (then a research-student in Trades Union studies) and for this child of the Welsh mining valleys. I barely restrained him from leaping to his feet and challenging the offending preacher. Being unaware of the history of Quakerism, I had no knowledge of the great wealth of precedent which there would have been for his action!

Coming Home

By 1980 I was training teachers and was a college lecturer both in Religious Studies and in what was coming to be known as multi-cultural education. That year we both encountered the Religious Society of Friends. I was not to know that in little more than a decade some writers would be pointing to 1980 as a kind of watershed year in modern Quakerism. It would be seen as the year when it 'came out' and showed itself in new colours, through Janet Scott's Swarthmore Lecture What Canst Thou Say?: towards a Quaker theology. 'A significant event' wrote Alastair Heron;[3]

> Scott's Swarthmore lecture epitomizes contemporary Quaker theology by accurately reflecting both its diversity and its divergence from traditional Christian thought and early Quaker teaching

declared Martin Davie in the Abstract of his thesis on Quaker theology.[4] Here was a Christianity in which, seemingly, even the Christ of the Quaker understanding (who is not wholly synonymous with the Christ of the creeds) was marginalised, in which diversity within Quakerism was acknowledged and affirmed, and in which it was evident that post Manchester-conference liberalism was now firmly recognised as conservatism. We knew none of this. It is a mark both of my own naïvety and of the power of the culture of silence, which disguises so much, that it took me some years to discover it.

How did I encounter the Society? I visited a Meet the Quakers exhibition. I had announced smugly to my husband that I'd go and check it out, and if it was any good, I'd take along a few students ...! He came along too. The positive response was more immediate for him than it was for me, but they certainly seemed 'lovely people'.

We were nurtured by recommended reading such as George Gorman's 1973 Swarthmore Lecture The Amazing Fact of Quaker Worship and by Geoffrey Hubbard's Quaker by Convincement (1974).[5] The latter made it quite clear that Quakerism was diverse, and he added that Friends were, in his view, 'a little less than clear sighted about what our doctrinal anarchy stands for'. But that did not deter me. Then there were the Advices and Queries and George Fox's Journal, study groups and encounters with Friends in the North, at Easter Settlement at Cober Hill and elsewhere.

I came to know more, not least of those whose names (Fell, Fox and Penn) had graced the streets of my home town in Wales and of those Quakers who had given their name to that village of Quakers' Yard which was a stone's throw from the house where I had been born. I had always wondered about them, as I had about a poem we had read at school.

This was Alun Lewis's poem The Mountain Over Aberdare:[6]

From this high quarried ledge I see
The place for which the Quakers once
Collected clothes, my father's home,
Our stubborn bankrupt village sprawled
In jaded dusk beneath its nameless hills ...

I knew Aberdare. I even knew the mountain, but were there still Quakers? I had wondered. In Wales one of the tragedies of Quakerism has been its invisibility and the tendency for it to be defined and remembered in terms of what was and was lost (by emigration), rather than by what has continued to be. Until I left Wales I had never knowingly met a Quaker.

And now as I read and listened and looked at Quakerism, I thought I kept seeing strands which led me to something which is very important in my religious thinking. That is prophecy. I shall come back to it in the final chapter.

Babies and bathwater

In the pages above there are clues about where I am coming from. It is a background which gave me both a knowledge of conventional religiosity and things about it to reject. My subsequent history, which has brought me into contact with Baptists of all sorts (not to mention people of all religions and of none), has also taught me how ignorant I was of the tradition I first embraced and then abandoned. The fact was that the Baptist family was much more diverse and more colourful in its history and its membership than I had imagined. Who knows, had I known better, it might have been able to keep me in its fold without either side compromising itself ... but I doubt it.

They failed too. They had failed to challenge me on what I was making of them and their understanding of Jesus Christ and the spiritual path. Certainly I was on one, but it took me some years to discover that it wasn't the same one as the people with whom I shared the pews. Outwardly, in many respects, I wasn't too wide of it, which is probably why no one thought to ask questions.

I had been engaged in what our Friend from the Wirral, Chas Raws, once memorably described as 'spiritual karaoke'. Like many a karaoke singer, I wasn't even aware that what I was doing was a far cry from the songwriter's intention. I was just singing along, but very much in my own style, because I knew some at least of the words.

The experience suggested two lessons to me. Firstly that it is as well to understand something of that setting in which you are making your spiritual home. It is nurturing to know the richness of its history, the breadth of its spirituality and understanding of discipleship, and the variety of congregations it embraces. It is important to know what obligations to its life and witness your membership will bring. And there is an obligation on the part of the receiving group to teach.

Those who come are seekers. If there is no guidance to the contrary, some may easily be led astray by superficial similarities to things they know already. Or they may be too ready simply to latch on to what is congenial, with a sigh of relief. One may even hang a whole religious edifice of one's own creation on a few handy pegs which the space provides (I did that), and without anyone knowing, at first at least.

So there is an 'I wish I had known' element in the first lesson which I drew. Former Jews and former Roman Catholics have said similar things to me, regretting that they were deprived of their heritage because no one educated them fully in the riches of their birthright or their place of adoption. Had they known, they might have appreciated it more, made their own contribution to it and not have left it in such angst.[7]

Secondly, a broken relationship can leave a legacy of bitterness and disappointment, with blame apportioned firmly, and in the main, to the one we have now separated from. As a result, the forging of new religious links can become a running away from ... a determined distancing from ... things which perhaps were once meaningful to us, even nourishing. Or alternatively they may have been things we dismissed without ever properly understanding. 'Glad there are lots of things we can discard...' as Pleasaunce Holtom's song put it.

In late twentieth century Quakerism there is a danger that this 'escapism' will show itself in something which Alastair Heron identified succinctly, namely the (unrealistic) demands that

> no one should ever say anything that might cause me pain - I've had enough already

and that

> you should not use in your spoken ministry religious language that I thought I had escaped from.[8]

Things from the religious past should not be 'Aunt Sallys' to be knocked down as we flee and (blithely mixing metaphors) perhaps throw out babies with bathwater.

If I have managed (I hope) to avoid much of the last, it is perhaps because I have always tended to blame myself. And I am probably not far wrong. But then I do not think we should abandon the word 'guilt'.

chapter five

THE EXPEDIENT
AND THE EDIFYING:
QUAKERS & DISUNITY

S O HOW DOES A Baptist-turned-Quaker[1] react after seventeen years in which she has been making some attempt to learn more (and has barely scratched the surface) of the Quakerism which has taken her in? The answer is surely clear already: with certain reservations about the pace and direction of change within it in recent decades; and thus with some difficulties when faced with the task of writing about the transmission of faith and values.

In particular I fear (after seventeen years) for the future existence of British Quakerism in the outwardly unified form which presently we take for granted. In this chapter and the next, however, I shall be thinking about Quakerism and Christianity in particular.

It is symptomatic of the way my mind works that the kinds of things I want to say express themselves in New Testament language (although, as must be obvious already, I am prone to the odd detour into Judaism and Islam as well). Bear with me, while I take us into the realms of Saul (later Paul) of Tarsus, going off at tangents from time to time.

'All things are lawful for me'

'All things are lawful' wrote Paul to the squabbling Christians of Corinth. But then he also added, 'not all *things are expedient'. To prod his point home he went on 'all things are lawful for me, but not all things are edifying' (I Corinthians 10:23 cf 6:12). One of those things which were not edifying, that is, did not 'build up' the group, was the flaunting of one's religious 'freedom' ('all things are lawful ...') at the expense of sensitivity to others.*

The Christian community in Corinth was probably not a large one. Christianity, in the 50's of the first century CE, was a very minor cult, not yet even illicit, and (to the Greco-Roman world) not obviously different from Judaism. The Corinthian Christian community would have comprised a number of house-churches and in his letter to them Paul was asking for sensitivity in the light of the diversity among them. The issues were traditionalism versus 'modernism'; a kind of legalism versus a liberal (but not libertarian) abandonment of 'externals'. Sometimes I think of this language when I fear that the 'freedom' of late twentieth century Quakerism may be in danger of treading unedifyingly on the certainties, the convictions, of some who remain within it.

In Corinth Christians were not treading softly on the dreams and experiences of their brothers and sisters. 'All things are lawful for me' could be a joyful rallying-cry for some, a kind of 'glad there are lots of things we can discard'. Christians had, after all, been told that the requirements of Torah (mediated through Moses) were no longer binding on them in the same way as they were upon Jews. For some this would have come as a liberation. But not all Christians, it should be said, agreed that it was so, or wanted it to be. The freedom from such 'externals', which some greeted gleefully, was in danger of being exercised at the expense of others, and to the detriment of the community as a whole.

This sentiment 'all things are lawful for me' was echoed by George Fox and other early Friends. The Friends of Truth were not 'under the Law' but walked in the Spirit (Romans 6:15; Galatians 5:18). At the same time Quakers (like Christians generally) have always acknowledged that the law of the Spirit (Romans 8:2; 2 Corinthians 3:6; Galatians 5:16-18) operated. For Friends it was operating in a guided individual life within a guided community of Friends, and it was intended to ensure (as was Torah for the Jews) that our relationships with God, with each other in a faith community, and with the wider world were not marred. So there was discipline.

Indeed as the Friends of Truth became organised into a coherent group there were fearful sideways glances at any hint of an 'anything goes' mentality, and at that 'Ranter spirit' which had provided an example of what might (and should not) happen.[2] Quakerism did become overly prescriptive in some periods of its history, but it has often preferred the discomforting query to the command, believing that its Meetings and experienced Friends had some idea of what a guided individual should look like.

'One gets the feeling', Gerald Priestland wrote,

> that instead of commanding 'Thou shalt not commit adultery' a Quaker Moses would have asked embarrassingly: 'Do you commit adultery?'[3]

The Friends of Truth movement organised itself (not without opposition from within) so as to avoid being an incoherence of individualists. It tried to temper excessive enthusiasm, and claims to fresh truth or knowledge, with obedient response to the upholding, testing, encouragement and censuring in the Meetings. Freedom, therefore, was not unfettered. They explained it (and I believe that they understood it, though some present-day Friends are more cynical about our ancestors) in terms of response to the leading of God.

Sometimes, I do not doubt, they got it wrong. Sometimes the Spirit was quenched by the 'worldly' intrusion of power-politics into religion, and it was thwarted by individuals' desire for control or lack of that faith which can countenance a leap in the dark ('live adventurously').[4]

Sometimes the most vociferous would have won the day. But the principle held good, even if at times it was betrayed in the practice.

Given guidance, discipline and mutual love, the fact that 'all things are lawful' would not bring degeneration into disorder or insensitivity.

'Not all things are expedient...'

In our own time we are seeing some concern that it is not just 'doctrines' of Quakerism which are changing but that discipline in the Religious Society of Friends is being eroded. An individualistic 'all things are lawful for me' is calling into question not only the existence, or rightness, of any limits for diversity but also the role of the 'gathered' Meeting. The truth of this assertion is verified not just by occasional letters in The Friend but also by the findings of academic observers of the Society in recent years.

Michael J Sheeran, an American researcher whose findings are of interest for British Quakerism too, wrote that what distinguishes Friends and Meetings is 'those who have experienced a gathered Meeting and those who have not'.[5] This is more worrying, it seems to me, than the christocentric-universalist divide, for it is the mode of discernment, the method of our Meetings which provides what (little though significant) unity we have. The Society's distinctive method of 'discernment', the researchers tell us, is a key element in Quaker cohesion.[6]

A threat to this latter would be a threat indeed. Individualism in doctrinal matters is one thing, we might say. Martin Davie wrote of:

> The axiomatic acceptance of the Liberal Quaker beliefs that Quakers should reinterpret Quakerism to fit in with contemporary thought and should have the freedom to do this as they see fit has meant that Quakers have felt free to develop their own thinking without feeling the need to defer to any kind of Quaker orthodoxy.[7]

And Alastair Heron noted that 'most contemporary Quakers' are open about their individual approach to life. But he also went on to say that:

> some at least of our local meetings extend that individualism into the corporate domain, not even treating the contents of Church Government as guidelines.[8]

That is something else. Ben Pink Dandelion's study and that of Caroline Plüss offered similar observations, the former warning of 'the desire to vote' and of 'the potential redundancy of the behavioural creed', while a study made in 1993 and entitled What are our Monthly Meetings Doing? A Concern for Revitalization of Meetings for Business 1992-1993 also told of individualism in business Meeting practice.[9]

Here then, is the tension between, on the one hand, perceptions of 'lawfulness' and, on the other hand, what is expedient and of spiritual worth for the Society. It brings us to what one writer in The Friend described as the critical division. Jim Dimond, in his piece 'Tension and Creation' (May 3rd, 1996) wrote of this being:

> between those who recognise the primacy and importance of the gathered Meeting and those who do not.

I agree with this view of the 'critical division'. Theological divides do have a part in making Meetings for worship and for business more fraught.[10] The Meeting is the forum in which as individuals and as a group we seek to encounter God/the Good (or whatever). But the Meeting is also the setting for our distinctive decision-making process. So diversity with regard to the nature and function of the Meeting (whether engendered by christocentric/universalist emphases or other things) can not be edifying.

The Quaker wheel

If it is the case, that 'the primacy and importance of the gathered Meeting' has been undermined, why has this been happening? Theological differences about God and discernment must surely have a part, but also, Jim Dimond went on, 'We are no longer close-knit in the way that our predecessors were' and 'The old commitments are no longer there'. New Friends (despite what he said was the care taken by visitors when they applied for membership) do not necessarily, or quickly, understand Quaker structures and practices. The analogy for a Meeting which he chose was that of the bicycle wheel.

Such a wheel has a rim and tyres or in the case of Quakerism 'Friends and Attenders who are not yet fully gathered' because they haven't had the time or, sometimes, the inclination to absorb fully the Quaker insights which lie at the hub.

As the wheel needs a strong hub, so Meetings need a strong centre, a truly gathered group. The whole is comprised of the centre in creative tension - like spokes - with the rim. In that way there is balance and effectiveness.

I thought of a danger which he had not named, but perhaps he too had it in mind; namely that those from the rim may find themselves too quickly in the role of the hub without clear understanding of, or even sympathy with, its long-standing function. What he did say was that with all the elements (the stimulus of new people, the strength and reliability at the core, the creative tension between the two) Meetings, and the Society *as a whole* will be healthy. Without them, 'we shall become Ranters or Quietists, or shall simply disintegrate'.

Balance was the key word - between stability and change, between ill-considered modifications which erode the significance of our practices and the need for innovation.

Margaret Heathfield had made the point clearly on page 109 of her 1994 Swarthmore Lecture *Being Together*, and she seemed to be writing about going too far:

> When we take actions such as opening our membership more widely, encouraging relatively inexperienced Friends to take responsibility in our life together, shortening periods of service or encouraging special interest groups, we are implicitly choosing the route towards a religious movement

(this is by contrast with a people of God) and 'making it more frustrating for ourselves when we try to speak with a united voice'. Each step needs to be understood in terms of the implicit choice we are making, 'otherwise we will find that we have gone so far down one route that there is no easy way back'.

I shall stay with this theme for a few paragraphs more, before getting back to Paul's language to the Corinthians.

From the Hub to the Core

Contrast the following two letters in The Friend. The first is from the issue of June 30th 1995.

This writer takes for granted the role of the 'gathered' Meeting in determining a God-ordained way forward for the group, while noting that 'different ways of expressing the core of the Society's belief may develop'. Was it not odd, however, that *we seem to have lost the idea of having a core belief ... in our worship and business meetings we traditionally seek unity. In reaching unity or 'gatheredness' we are assured of the authenticity of the experience. Inconsistently, in basic matters of faith we seem to take disunity as a sign of strength. We call it diversity.*

Was the Society 'too readily accepting the materialism and individualism of the age'? the writer asked. Were Friends, he wondered, 'losing all sense of mission, and rejecting even the hope of finding some clear aspect of truth that demands our loyalty'. If so, 'then we are indeed facing in the opposite direction to the Society's founders'.

A response in The Friend of the following week was revealing. The aforementioned writer, it said

raises issues which lie at the heart of the Society's view of itself ... to entirely subordinate one's light to a corporate light is to surrender to the authority of the Church, whether it calls itself Catholic or Quaker ... those who urge subordination of individual to corporate judgement ... usually do so to control dissent.

This was uncompromising stuff. In any case, this second writer seemed to suggest, the battle - if such it was - was lost, even in Quakerism's own terms. For advocates of 'one Truth' Quakerism should ponder the fact that

if, as now seems to be the case, it is the corporate judgement of the Society that diversity in matters of faith is a strength rather than a weakness, isn't there a touch of 'ranterism' in dissenting from a position to which the Society seems to have been led?

In other words diversity in matters of belief is Quaker orthodoxy, a view borne out by the sociologists' findings.

And its corollary, to judge from R W Lee's studies of Unitarian universalists (as quoted by Ben Pink Dandelion) is that liberal beliefs 'centred as they are on the individual, simply do not encourage ... subordination of individual interests to those of the group'.[11]

Ranters and traditionalists

A Ranterish traditionalism (an interesting but perhaps necessary oxymoron) does exist, nevertheless. In one form it dares even to suggest that the Society is lacking in integrity. Integrity is a good word, as it indicates a wholeness unmarred by failure to include necessary elements. The 'Ranterish' traditionalism was expressed bluntly, and evidently following years of wrestling with the matter, in a small item by T Roy Dutton in The Friend of April 5th 1996, under the title 'A House Divided'. He wrote as follows:

> Worship-sharing on the strengths, weaknesses and growing points of our Meetings brings to some a sense of futility, remembering how in the past these exercises had mostly served to reveal the major differences in belief and priority between us.

The heart of the matter was that for some Friends ('for many of us') the honouring of Jesus 'as the supreme source and inspiration of Quaker faith and practice is not an optional element of Friends' beliefs'.

Roy Dutton had been focused on the words of the letter to the Hebrews, 12:1-2, where believers were told to strip off encumbrances, 'as well as the sin which dogs our feet', so as to run the race with patience, eyes fixed on Jesus, 'the source and goal of our faith'. It seemed to me that the language of sin here, of Jesus and of the goal of our faith was surely just what would provoke and draw attention to the 'major differences in belief and priority' of which he had been writing. It is the language of the Society's previous convictions and the language of present conviction for only some Quakers. Then there followed (were they a challenge or a plea?) these words:

> If many others within Britain Y(early) M(eeting) feel it has become so [ie an optional element], there seems no honest option but to acknowledge that we have become a hopelessly compromised and apostacized branch of the Christian church, and to disband and possibly re-form, with the integrity which currently seems to elude us.

A re-forming, it should be said, exists already, among the small number of plain Quakers now associated with the Yearly Meeting of the Friends in Christ (formed 1993). Issue no. 1 of its journal, The Call, for 1996, laid out the causes for its now separated state (separated, that is, from Britain Yearly Meeting). These included the Society having lost sight of its original ideals and its character as the Church of which Christ is head. They included dismay at the acceptance into membership, in the name of 'tolerance', of 'many people' who are atheists. They included allowing the testimonies of Friends 'for which our Quaker forefathers suffered and died' to become matters of personal conscience and for some 'optional'. They included condemnation of 'the insipid travesty' by which Friends' understanding of 'that of God in every man' has become no longer the revelation of Christ in all of us but rather 'understood widely as a little bit of niceness in everyone'. Consequently (and echoing 2 Corinthians 6:14) 'we cannot be yoked together in BYM with some of its members'.

During the weeks which followed T Roy Dutton's letter in The Friend I awaited the spate of responses in the Letters pages. There was not total silence. There was one.

'Not all things build up...'

Getting back to the 'edification' language of Paul the Apostle, I try to be optimistic. I do not think it is yet a commonplace amongst Friends that their historical witness to the possibility and rightness of corporate judgement, when 'gathered' and guided, is to be presented as a misguided excuse to quash dissent. This is not to say, of course, that some Friends do not regard it that way or that the methodology of our Meetings is never used, and wrongly, to that end, and for expediency's sake![12] But it seems to me an absolute necessity for the edification of our Meetings that those within them should understand what the Quaker witness with regard to such things actually has been.

It is certainly becoming a recurring theme of Swarthmore Lectures, of research into Quakers and in comment by Friends, that such understanding is not to be taken for granted.[13] This, as I've said, is the unedifying (and I think crucial) division in the Society - between (A) those who understand and acknowledge the primacy of the gathered Meeting and (B) those who do not. This is a major challenge for the Society in its keeping of faith, its expression of faith and its transmission of faith.

Yet the Society itself pays greater attention to the so-called christocentric vs universalist Friends divide, perhaps because some of the protagonists are vociferous and the language unedifying.[14] This is not to be ignored, although the universalist-christocentric labels may in fact mislead. Each is open to a variety of definitions and some Friends would regard themselves as neither (but as something else) or as embracing an element of both (I include myself in this category). The difference can be real, however. And occasionally feelings run high on both sides. At times the word 'offence' is used, and honestly. Sometimes the language is interesting:

> Friends in Britain ... are increasingly expressing
> the necessity of dragging Quakerism into the
> twenty-first century with a change of emphasis
> in theology ... the uncomfortable truth is that 'pain'
> ... is the inevitable consequence of change, of
> growth, and of evolving maturity ... the 'offence'
> taken by some Friends is an 'offence' given to
> others.[15]

Rightly Adrian Cairns (the writer quoted above) tells us that the change is 'often spearheaded (forgive the old phrase!) by those with universalist attitudes',[16] while by contrast 'in answer to the increasing pace of change' there is currently

> a defensive and conservative wave of traditional
> Christian witness, among Quakers as among other
> branches of a beleaguered Christian Church.[17]

I confess that I find this terminology intriguing. Does the 'spearheading' imply something more than an 'old phrase'? Does it indeed imply an attack against which defence is necessary, and that some manifestations of diversity in Quakerism are more acceptable than others? Which Friends are 'increasingly' wanting to drag others? I have an interest in these questions, for it is my previous (and present) convictions at which the spears are aimed. And the threat of being dragged promises an odd sensation.

Clearly I have got this Quakerism business wrong again. I had assumed that it was people like me, the former Baptist ('we'll have you back, fach', promises my colleague who is principal of a Baptist theological college - 'you'll be alright, at least you're baptised' teases my Anglo-Catholic colleague with a smile), who speak still of convincement, who have not abandoned the language of faith and tradition, who were the alleged perpetrators of 'one Truth Quakerism'.

In another respect I was not wrong, I think. It really is hard, at the end of the twentieth century, to write with ease and conviction about the transmission of Quaker faith and values.

chapter six

MANNERS AND
THE MEAT MARKET

So ... I AM AN INCOMER. *I am an incomer who over time in the Religious Society of Friends has come to worry about liberty and expediency, group identity and a possible erosion of the cohesion which is born of shared values. Some of my difficulties in meeting the task of writing about faith and values have come because of this: I have not yet found anything among us which is replacing satisfactorily for the Society the Christian language and assumptions in which the Society's roots formerly had a firm anchor. This chapter, then, concerns de-Christianization.*

'Do not destroy'

First I want to recall a less-quoted utterance of Paul, from his letter to the Romans 14:14-15 and v 20 (cf 1 Corinthians 8:4-13). Put plainly, Paul wrote (v 15):

> do not destroy with your meat the one for whom Christ died.

'Do not destroy with your meat ...' was a saying about freedom and responsibility. It was Paul's warning about despising scrupulosity, well-tried understandings of the faith, and the tender conscience. It was at odds with an 'I know better' pragmatic response to 'the world', which was being defended by appeal to that freedom which the Christian religion accorded, and which saw itself as 'mature' ('pain' is 'the inevitable consequence ... of evolving maturity', wrote Adrian Cairns in the booklet quoted in the previous chapter).

Paul knew all about Christian diversity. The problem was that some, on one wing of the diverse, were dismissing for 'primitive legalism' other people's reliance on what they continued to experience as the command of God. It was perhaps for them akin to what Adrian Cairns called 'rigidity enforced by old forms and old language … stunting growth'. They wanted very much to drag Christians into the second half of the first century.

Paul's words to the Corinthians were a warning. There was to be no triumphalist rejoicing at being given freedom, even if that seemed to allow one to jettison the requirements of one's past religious observance. It could prove to be the discomforting of others, who were no less in the light of God. In Paul's day, of course, some had come into Christianity without ever having experienced, or valued, the scrupulous obligations which a religion might impose. They were not to impose their understanding, said Paul, on the faithful whose consciences were nourished by a different, and well-tried, understanding of the demand of God. It is a view I find among some Friends, who have never known the challenge and joy of more traditional religious living and who feel assured that those who do are in need of being relieved of it.

Paul was well acquainted with Christians who tended to think of themselves as spiritually more insightful than other Christians and who were not dependent, they thought, on 'crutch' traditional religiosity. Indeed he used language which reflected the labels which the groups applied to one another: 'weak' was one of them, and 'strong' another.[1] The new religion of Christianity, as the strong interpreted it, left them free to disregard the externals of belief and practice which others held to, and (in a setting where what you ate mirrored what you were in religious terms) to eat whatsoever they pleased without querulousness.

Today, as then, some might think that a view of religion which demythologises, rationalises, humanises and minimalises is preferable, given humanity's greater 'knowledge'. 'Our human task' wrote David Boulton in The Friend of May 24th 1996, 'is not to discover some absolute standard independent of us, but to work out together, in reason and good conscience, right and wrong ways of living together ...'[2] But the strong, wrote Paul, exacted a high price in terms of relations with their 'weaker' Christian brothers and sisters, who might well have argued that they represented loyalty to an understanding of faith and the faith which was more original and no less liberating. It rather depends on what one wants to be liberated from and liberated for.

The Meat Market

What was all this about? The meat sold in the marketplaces throughout the Roman empire had commonly made its first appearance on the sacrificial slab of some local temple, dedicated to one deity or another. It was, as Paul and other Jews put it, 'meat sacrificed to idols'. Other foods may also have passed through as offerings (1 Corinthians 8:1,4,10; cf Acts 15:28f; 21:25; Revelation 2:14 and 20).

Strictly monotheistic Jews (including some who were now converts to Christianity) would have nothing to do with it, and their own rites of meat preparation would have precluded them using it. But Paul (formerly a Jew of Pharisaic type, he claimed: Acts 23:6, 26:5; Philippians 3:5) was now on the side of the liberals. Indeed he was of the opinion that eating meat previously used as an offering to idols made no difference - idols had no reality anyway (1Corinthians 8:4-8). On the other hand, he knew of Christian people who could not bear to touch it and who wouldn't have wanted to sit down to dinner with those who passed it around the table. So despite his own tendencies on the matter, Paul insisted that the consciences and obedience of some should not be compromised because of the 'liberty' flaunted by the others.

The liberals were warned 'do not destroy with your meat the one for whom Christ died'. Though they felt they had moved beyond the vestiges of a 'religion of the letter', with its abstinence from bloody meat, running parallel with their freedom there was a danger. It was the danger of a neo-orthodoxy of ultra-liberalism, and of insensitivity to the experience and faith of others.

In this case, of course, both sides were clearly and avowedly Christian. Jesus Christ was the foundation for their faith. This was a debate about practice. The differences of practices related to how the effects of the work of this Jesus Christ were to be understood.

I thought of Paul's words as I saw the excision of Christian language from the new Book of Discipline. The bland and the seemingly deliberately ambiguous now stand in it, and while discipleship is still recommended, we are not to be told of what or of whom we are disciples.[3] The details of the changes have been rehearsed and regretted in print by quite a number of Friends, so there is no point in bemoaning the Society's response to some Friends' complaints, since 1960, about explicitly Christological language. But Chas Raws came to mind again. This bon mot related to discipleship (he had no idea that in meetings of CCIR and the Quaker Theology Seminar I was noting down his memorable language). 'When George Fox said that Christianity was not a notion but a way', Chas Raws observed, 'that didn't mean he had no notion of what it was.'

I wondered, nevertheless, whether this was a case of the liberty of some being bought at the price of sensitivity to others who continuéd to speak a language of Quakerism familiar for three hundred years rather than thirty. 'Signpost' words (still important for some, even if others choose to go a different way) were now removed. The public face of Quakerism was changed. But in the process, and worst of all, I came to feel (as the Welsh have done in the past) that 'they' had taken away my language.

'Intolerance of Christian ministry ...'

It is not true that Friends in the 1990's have no loyalty to the language and thought of Christianity. This is my second point in discussing de-Christianization, and I make it strongly, lest it be felt that I am accusing Friends en masse of having lapsed into New Ageism, neo-paganism and abandonment of all our historic testimonies. Many of us retain loyalty to language and tradition which is long established among Friends. But given Friends' testimony against the need for credal affirmations, it's unlikely that we shall have a census on the matter of who would call themselves Christian! We do not know how many.

Nevertheless the existence of the New Foundation Fellowship, which works to promote understanding of Quakerism's original insights, of the Christian Quaker Renewal Fellowship, with gatherings now advertised in The Friend for Christian fellowship and the fact that in the 1990's we have seen a small but not necessarily insignificant schism in the Society, with the creation of the Friends in Christ (is all this the 'defensive and conservative wave of traditional Christian witness...'?) suggest that it is not just my perception that 'traditional' language and belief needs to be affirmed. I am not a member of any of the groups concerned.

Some Friends, however, do report being challenged or made to feel uncomfortable when they offer ministry in Meeting which is couched in the language of Christianity or which affirms any of its teachings. Some have even been led to stop attending their local Meeting.

> I have stopped attending Meeting for Worship because two Friends who mentioned Christ in their ministry were both eldered. I am still a Quaker, of course.

That quotation came from a reply to Ben Pink Dandelion's research questions.[6] Similarly Joseph Pickvance has written of

> Intolerance of Christian ministry ... expressed after the Meeting or even during it. Although not common, this open intolerance is very widespread.[7]

This has never been my own experience in the four Meetings to which I've belonged. But conversations with Friends from other Meetings, and in other settings, do tell me that it exists. It is clear to me that the faith I have in mind as deserving of transmission is not shared, or regarded as Quakerly, by not a few Quakers.

On an even keel

It is not a matter of what 'brand' of Quakerism dominates numerically, though it is important that none of us is marginalised or left to feel powerless. The real power issue is about whether God and the guided Meeting has sovereignty in Quaker lives. But pluralism, unfettered, has its dangers, if there comes with it a fear of speaking out, through reticence lest we offend, or through fear of being criticised by others as illiberal, too radical or whatever.

The researchers tell us that we have devised strategies for minimising ministry-initiated conflict. Caroline Plüss, for example, reported that

> A speaker is expected to express points held in common with the previously articulated views of other speakers.[8]

Presumably the Friends she interviewed had told her that, remarkable though I find it. When our pluralism brings with it a desire at any cost not to rock the boat, but to keep our fragile craft on an even keel, then there will be no 'words of power'. Teresa Hobday wrote of pluralism as a Trojan horse, full of destructive and disintegrating powers:

> Our demise as a community of faith may be comfortable and pleasant, but the prophetic voice which discerns the truth and speaks it will fall silent and be heard no more.[9]

The prospect depresses me. The community, or family of faith, is an ideal I value. The prophetic voice is something I value too. It was because I believed I had found both in the Religious Society of Friends that I wanted to join it. I shall write about them in Part Two of *Previous Convictions*. I do not want them jeopardised.

This, then, has been my third point in respect of de-Christianisation of Quakerism (if that is what the latter half of this century has brought us). If we are to live with, grow from and prophesy out of pluralism, we must ensure that we do not jettison the integrity which comes of all being subject to Guidance. With what do we replace the language of Christian Quakerism, if we want to replace it?

Commas and Confusion
Writing this has made me confront myself. There are times, I realise, when I keep silent when I should be speaking. There are times when I choose not to 'rock the boat', against my own judgement. And increasingly I am confused about language, as I think the Society is confused. Let me start with the problem of commas.

From time to time I write variously about Quakers and for Quakers. Nowadays I encounter major problems of punctuation. The comma is crucial. When I write, for example, the words 'others who are Christians say ...' should it be instead 'others, who are Christians, say...'?

When talking with, or writing for, non-Quaker Christians (or do I mean non-Quakers, Christians) I am rarely challenged if I describe myself as a Christian who is a Quaker - give or take those few who believe that Friends are all neo-pagans anyway, or who could not bring themselves to regard anyone devoid of clergy and sacraments as Christian. The ecumenists can acknowledge the existence of such Quaker Christian creatures (a secondary danger is that Quakers are perceived as a body of unalloyed saintliness, trailing heritage clouds of good-works). A number of years of quite heavy involvement in Christian ecumenism has convinced me that they do not require me to juggle with the commas. But the dilemmas are real nevertheless. They are real especially when writing for a Quaker readership.

'Is it true,' asked the immensely likeable Joel Edwards, director of the Evangelical Alliance, 'that Quakerism is almost entirely New Age now?' I insisted that the Society was not so. But in truth can I any longer assert that its relation, corporately, to Christianity bears close resemblance to even that distinctive understanding of Christianity which characterised it in the past? I could speak only for where I stood. I confess uncertainty as to how the Religious Society of Friends corporately would choose to describe itself when challenged (and this despite sections 11.01 and 11.14 of the Book of Discipline, the meaning of which I cannot fathom[10]). I know, too, that there are some Friends (and I am certainly not one of them) who would say that 'speaking corporately' is not something which is desirable, let alone possible, for Quakerism in any case. So there I am - confused.

It seemed straightforward to the philosopher John Macmurray when he wrote the Swarthmore Lecture in 1965. 'I take it for granted', he said,

> I think rightly, that the Society of Friends is also Christian, and I often wish that we might feel constrained to proclaim ourselves not merely a religious but also a Christian Society of Friends.[11]

It is not so now. And so my commitment to Christian ecumenism is foundering - not on problems of working which (with wholesome honesty or not) has been designed to circumvent Quakers' rejection of credal language and to gain them entry into the ecumenical bodies - but on the rock of suspicion that I am 'representing' a Quakerism which in growing measure does not exist.

Worst of all, in dealings with Friends I too am falling prey to that defensiveness described by quite a number of the respondents to Ben Pink Dandelion's study. For a Quaker readership I have been descending into what I am coming to see as weasel words. I write about being 'liberal in theology' and (getting my retaliation in first) against possible accusations of narrowness and failure to be open to …'[12], I state my inter-faith credentials for good measure.

> Christine Trevett has taught Muslim teenagers in Saharan outposts, helped to establish the Inter-Faith Network in Wales, teaches religions X and Y and their related languages, is a member of the Council of Christians and Jews, once came close to marrying a Muslim, has seen the inside of more synagogues, mosques, gurdwaras etc than many have had hot dinners, numbers Buddhists, Unificationists ('Moonies'), Mormons, Rosicrucians and witches among her students, has had neighbours who brought her rice and mutton at Eid, some of her best friends …

I would not add that 'despite evidently being someone in a position to know better, she stubbornly describes herself as a Christian, when she could just be a Quaker …and no questions asked', but there have been moments when I wondered whether I should. I think I am developing a certain, and unQuakerly, paranoia.

This is not good. 'Self-censorship', fear of 'treading on toes', the 'culture of silence', fear of 'isolation' - all terms which in Sociological Analysis Ben Pink Dandelion used in the chapter on Change, are products of increased diversity and decreased trust and cohesion in the Religious Society of Friends. These are among the things which contribute to the demise of the words of power, of the prophetic voice, of the request for spiritual guidance and of the expression of what the individual has found. And these are the very things which are needed for the transmission of faith and values.

Yes!

I didn't realise how strongly I had come to feel about the things in this chapter until I found myself cheering (actually cheering, like my son, hand in air and crying 'YES!') while reading John Punshon's Swarthmore Lecture Testimony and Tradition. The book was such a far cry from the Christ-less Quakerism which some wish not just to embrace ('another redundancy at Friends House' mused Ben Pink Dandelion at a Quaker Theology Seminar meeting) but by degrees to make the norm, with regard to our language at least.

It spoke about certainties of a kind which increasingly in some Friends' circles seem to be marginalised, rejected or taken as synonymous with bigotry. It was not that I would normally have used the language that John Punshon used - though I'm familiar enough with it. In fact it makes me ill-at-ease. It was that in the context of 1990's British Quakerism it seemed an act of considerable courage and witness to use it.

Further on in the lecture he wrote of holding to certainties which are met with amazement and incomprehension, not to mention the assumption of his naïvety. His language echoed the words of the book of Revelation, of the slain but triumphant Lamb of God. What he had written was this:

> I carry the cross because the Lamb carried the cross, not because we are both examples of an abstract carrying of the cross in some platonic form or Jungian archetype. I know the Lamb, so I trust to his victory.[13]

And I found myself cheering.

chapter seven

LOOSE ENDS

THIS CHAPTER OF Previous Convictions brings to an end Part One of the book. It brings together some of the things which have been mentioned already. It also concerns thinking, the unthinkable and pick and mix combinations. Some confessions remain. I have to admit to an intolerance of 'melting-pot' beliefs and practices and of what John Punshon described as the 'supermarket' approach to faith.[1] I may as well. The Swarthmore lecturer has no place to hide - the truth is out. I also have to admit to advocating that we resurrect words which will make some Friends blush. Among them are pontificate, proselytise and evangelise.

Searching the depths

In May of 1996 I had completed Part One of this book. In June I bought from the Quaker Bookshop the just-published work Searching the Depths: essays on being a Quaker today,[2] and I found that some others in the Society were articulating what I was feeling.

The essays in it told of Friends who do not accept the necessity for 'a wholly voluntary self-discipline of the spiritual life' and of a 'go it alone' approach in Meetings. It said that there needed to be sharing of findings and arrivings rather than pride in 'permanent search and an endless voyage' and that British Quakers were now becoming too content with the method and the process, without necessarily understanding the basis for either.

When Andrew Greaves called for more tenacious mental activity amongst Friends,[3] so as to reflect upon our religious experience ('take an interest in theological issues'), I sensed an exasperation like my own, with a superficial bandying of 'Light' and 'that of God' language, without there being desire to explore, define and articulate in a way which others may understand. I too had believed there was a danger that some Friends may become endless collectors of data, experts in comparative religion, even; making a virtue of being perpetual seekers rather than tackling head-on a question which is fundamental to our religious journey.

Reticence and fear of rejection were there too. Elizabeth Barnett told of inability to share our deepest encounters, which is 'an indicator of the poverty of our spiritual lives'. The fact was that we were not overjoyed when our spiritual paths crossed. Instead we tended to eye one another with suspicion, examining each other's passports and criticising each other's maps.

Looking at all this I remembered one response recorded by Ben Pink Dandelion in his study Sociological Analysis:

> Quakerism is the M25 of religions - four lanes of traffic whizzing round in circles in both directions, waving at each other.[4]

In the same book Jean Hardy ('Why am I a Quaker?') looked to Buddhism for 'the depth of the teaching', and found in 'the freedom' of Quaker gatherings the 'lovely people' which my broadcaster friend had recognised too. But while for him it was our 'relentless optimism' which alienated him, for the universalist Jean Hardy it is 'the element of traditionalism ... piousness in the Society' which is difficult.[5] Finally in David Boulton, an attender and activist in the Sea of Faith movement, the iconoclastic debunking of Quaker 'golden-ageism' involved describing seventeenth century Quaker diversity and clashes of personality. As an occasional historian of seventeenth century Friends I also recognise and acknowledge these, but not what David Boulton extrapolated from the picture, namely that not only may we not now speak of Truth, but that Quakerism never could.[6] For him

> earlier Quaker generations cobbled together a one Truth they could witness to ... which could be maintained only by discipline.[7]

Searching the Depths, then, offered as good an introduction to the dilemmas and diversities of 1990's Quakerism as I had come across, and at points touched on many of the issues in Previous Convictions. My relief that some others felt the same as I did was tempered by a feeling that perhaps much of 'it' had been said already!

The Quaker amoeba

At times in the preceding chapters I have been talking about myself. It will be clear by now that I believe some searching of the depths is necessary, for pre-new millennium Quakerism to determine the what and why of its being. Without such determination it can neither present itself adequately to the world nor transmit coherently faith and values in its own ranks. What is this thing called Quakerism? I am no longer certain that I know. I am clearer about our previous convictions than about our present ones. In this portion of 'Loose Ends', then, I am touching on some alternative models of Quakerism which I've observed.

Here is one view: I recall a Friend at a meeting of the Committee for Christian and Interfaith Relations (of which I was a member at that time) responding exasperatedly to understandable objections about Quaker involvement in Christian ecumenism. Her words were 'if we don't belong in the ecumenical movement [the council of churches], where do we belong? The council of mosques?' The question challenged an implied assumption that Quakerism was so 'other', so separated from the rock out of which it was hewn, so independent a religion, that it would be as valid to say 'I am not a Christian, I'm a Quaker' (as indeed some do) as to say 'I'm not a Hindu, I'm a Rastafarian'. So, the argument might run, the major ecumenical 'umbrella' groups are not for us. We are 'something different'.

Quakerism may of course legitimately be paralleled with many a tendency in the world of religion – and with different ones at different times in its history – prophetism, Quietism, mysticism and more. But radically to estrange it from Christianity in the process is a new development, I think. Whenever Quakerism has been regarded as heresy, or as irritating grit for the pearl of justice and reform, or even (as W R Inge said) as the one body which 'remained nearest to the teaching and example of Christ', it was assumed to have its relations within the Christian family.[8] Deeply sectarian as it has been, it has not seen itself as a separate religion. Heresy can only be a family affair.

Arguably some Friends would want to say that now it is not a matter of nonalignment but of different alignment. We are indeed something else. But is it any one thing? For some it will be alignment with the thought of Buddhism, for others alignment with pantheistic modes of thinking which mesh well with 'green' activism and so on. This leaves me with many questions unanswered in my mind.

Is Quakerism a phenomenon of limitless diversity? Or are there indeed limits to our plurality already? Some which we would like to see imposed? If so why? What would they be? On what criteria would they be determined? Now there's an exercise for a study group! What are the implications of Friends' plurality for the language we use, for the process of 'discernment' in our Meetings and (very important) for the tasks which corporately we would want to undertake (our social witness) and which are undertaken in our name?

Then there is the individualism-congregationalism model. If Quakerism increasingly is being defined in terms of what the individual Meeting, or individual Friend, determines that it is, then will Quakerism, which might come to embrace everything, cease to be anything very much? Will we be speaking only of the ill-defined, shifting and amoeba-like, altering its character on each contact? I wondered about this after the case of the Lammas rites in an English Meeting House.

News of this brought me up against the reality of Quaker pluralism to a degree I'd not encountered before. What struck me was not that some assumed I was an illiberal condemner of communing with nature, but that there was little comprehension of, or interest in, dilemmas arising from this situation which had nothing to do with unfettered tolerance of other people's spiritual paths.

Those Friends who regretted having missed the rites of offering corn to the Goddess in a Meeting House had no thought for (seemingly in some cases no knowledge of) the Society's previous convictions and testimonies with regard to externals ('the outward'). Such things concerned liturgy and ritual, times and seasons, priesthood, dependence on God, or whatever (for magical rites assume control rather than dependence), or exclusivity (in this case single-sex rites). These matters seemingly had no place in the discussion at all. But I did muse whether the same Lammas-loving Friends would have moved with alacrity to join in if it had been the local Anglicans celebrating Eucharist in the same Meeting House.

Did this mean that Quakerism had no identity to speak of beyond its willingness to align itself with just about anything in the whole world of belief? Certainly this was quite a different model of Quakerism from the one I thought I knew. I thought I'd attached myself to a different beast altogether, but there was that amoeba again.

White water adventure

We must never lose our openness to the Spirit. But here is a confession about what this Quaker sometimes finds herself doing in Meetings for worship. I am thinking - an activity well suited to the quenching of the Spirit. I warm to the story told of the nineteenth century Quaker and mystic Rufus Jones being 'eldered' by William Graham of Birmingham. Rufus Jones had begun a spoken ministry with the words 'I was thinking', to receive the rebuke

> I was grieved at what thou said in Meeting. Thou said that since sitting in the Meeting thou hadst been thinking. Thou shouldst not have been thinking.[9]

This is a particularly 19th century view of behaviour in Meeting, but one well suited to someone like me, I think, who spends too much time being rhetorical about religion and garrulous about God.

I do degenerate into thinking, as on the occasion when I was at a Meeting where Donald Southall, BYM's Recording Clerk, was ministering - a man who will forgive me, I'm sure. Our spiritual journey, he was saying, may be exhilarating, adventurous. As in white-water canoeing we may find ourselves tossed about and experience the unpredictability of the wind-Spirit. Life propelled by the Spirit is not dull. It is true! It is true in my experience too. So why could I not quell the thought that kept surfacing in my mind? 'Ah yes', my Self was saying, 'but are we all in the same boat? And is it called Quakerism?'[10]

A friendly society

Here is another model. For some Quakers the word 'religious' is a stumbling block. They would prefer to see the term 'Religious' dropped entirely from the title Religious Society of Friends. I have never understood why this should be. Probably I have not met the best advocates of this idea, for those I have talked with seem only to be expressing a generalised ill-ease with the word.

To erase it would certainly erase associations with 'the others', Christians, Muslims and so on. It would also, I suppose, disassociate Quakers from those 'negative' things (discipline? accountability to God? belief systems? the uncongenially challenging? the judgemental? certainty?) which 'religious' implies for some people. I suspect, too, that Society of Friends sounds nice because it does indeed have overtones of the pleasantly philanthropic and open. I once belonged to a Meeting which was listed in the phone book under *Society of Friends* and which received phone calls from the isolated and elderly who were looking for a club promoting contact and friendship (which is among the things we do too, of course). The 'religious', however, was not what they had in mind.

The Latin word *religio* was used in a number of ways during the many centuries of its common usage. One meaning was that of 'ordering'. *Religio* was the making sense of nonsense, the bringing of order out of seeming chaos. Another was that of binding. There are constraints in religion, containments and borders. There are shared assumptions and values which bind together those who belong. Societies may operate in similar ways, but for me what distinguishes Quakerism from membership of the golf club or the local history group is that the binding agent is not a shared recreational interest or a setting in which friendships may be fostered, but rather that it is a shared reliance upon Something greater, which gives to us the liberation of order, and which does constrain and bind us. The society (small 's') which we are is a religious one, I hope.

Perhaps the Friends who want the term 'religious' erased are simply asking that language catches up with reality. In the light of answers to his questionnaire

Alastair Heron characterised the Society as 'the doubtfully religious Society of very friendly individualists'.[11] And a Society of Friends (minus Religious) certainly sounds like a place where 'lively' people are. Nevertheless I confess that I find the idea very unappealing indeed. Perhaps it is because I regret 'niceness'.

Niceness is at odds with the prophetic, and it was the prophetic which brought me into the Society (see Part Two). The realm of God is not 'nice'. Challenging, dangerous, exhilarating when encountered, joy-inducing, discomforting, bringing disorientation and more (like white-water canoeing), but nothing so bland as 'nice' in my experience. The word 'religious' is a reminder of whose realm we are thinking about.

A gleam in a Welshman's eye

The phrase 'religious society of friends' was a gleam in a Welshman's eye long before it became shining reality as the title of our Society. That gives me another reason for liking it. In seventeenth century Wales, as elsewhere in the land, there were many troublesome and dissenting preachers who had tilled that ground into which the seeds from the Friends of Truth fell. One of the most significant was William Erbery. His family came to be associated with that same village of Quakers Yard (though that was not then its name) which was a stone's throw from my birthplace. His daughter Dorcas was one of the associates of James Nayler, in the infamous messianic-style ride into Bristol in 1656.[12]

But William, 'plundered' minister, much travelled preacher and father of the Seekers died in 1654, before either his daughter's disgrace or the coming of the Friends of Truth to South Wales. His sermons on the poor, on social injustice, tithes and clergy wrongs had much in common with the Friends' teaching, and Cardiff 'convincements' probably owed a lot to William Erbery's congregation. Part of his vision for the future of religion was that there would emerge truly a 'religious society of friends'.[13]

Emporium, counselling and call

All kinds of models of Quakerism are in the air. For myself, I continue to believe that Quakerism is something, is a religious Society and that we may jeopardise it if we assume too readily that anything and everything can be embraced within its motherly arms without extending these too far for well being.

What it is, as I see it, has continuity, in many respects, with its previous self. It is not for me to remake it in my own image or conform it (like the incomers and aboriginals I referred to in chapter one) to what is congenial to myself. It is I who must be conformed by it, by the Spirit at work not least in its Meetings. These are the things the reader must have in mind when reading Part Two of Previous Convictions.

Certainly I have no qualms about being informed by the insights of other Christian (or other, Christian) denominations and by the examples of inspiring individuals from many faiths and of none. I have never warmed to the vapid witticism from Monsignor Ronald Knox some decades ago, which ran 'comparative religion makes people comparatively religious' (though indeed this may prove true of individuals). It would certainly be a very unQuakerly stance to claim the monopoly of insight. From the days of Mary Fisher and William Penn, Robert Barclay and John Woolman, we can find witnesses to Friends' openness to 'the promptings of truth and love' as evidenced in the hearts of people quite different from themselves. We can find from those times a Quaker view of the 'catholic' (= universal) Church which speaks of a commonality of inward transformation such as may be found among peoples of all faiths. This is different from

Catholic allegiance to doctrines of apostolic succession or the need for ordained male hierarchies. One does not have to carry a label such as 'Quaker universalist' to continue to hold to such truths.

But recognising the universal applicability of 'Quaker' truths is one thing. It is surely not the same as assuming that Quakerism becomes no less Quakerism, is unchanged or improved, by selected and diluted additions of truths characteristic of Buddhism, Sufism, Adlerian psychology, native American Indian theology or whatever, and to varying degrees from Meeting to Meeting, Friend to Friend. Being informed by is quite different from being conformed to, or seeking to conform Quakerism to such things.

Here I stand. Quakerism, I dare to say (and it will not make me popular amongst a considerable number of Friends) is not Buddhism, transactional analysis (or is that passé now?) or synonymous with the world-view of the Labour Party (of which I am a member). It is not a less demanding substitute for Judaism - though it is where many Friends can take a 'Jewish' unitarian stance. I may well have gained from the insights of such religions from time to time, but I do not live the life (life and 'in the Life', not 'lifestyle') of them. If I did, then would I not be a Buddhist or a Jew? Evidently I am not a person who believes of the world's religious traditions that 'we all believe the same things really'. No we don't, though we may certainly learn from one another.

So among the 'loose ends' of my own thinking which I am tying up are some threads which interweave with John Punshon's 1990 Swarthmore Lecture.

There he wrote of the emporium or supermarket approach to Quaker faith:

> selecting from the shelves whatever nourishment one chooses, with very little restriction. The tins and packets in the trolley do not need to add up to a consistent or balanced diet.

Coherence was not an issue. Supermarket Quakerism simply dispensed with the idea that the testimonies were each part of a greater whole from which they derived their cogency, and that there was 'a basis for them which is not necessarily sympathetic to the presuppositions of rationalism and humanism'.[14] The same also holds true, of course, with respect to the other religions from which 'pickings' are taken. This tends to be done without regard for that greater whole which gives them their cogency.

But this had come about, John Punshon suggested, because increasingly Quakerism was a 'needs centred movement'.

Brand loyalty and niche marketing

Before I go on, all the loyalists of Adler, transactional analysis etc whom I have offended already should please understand what I am not saying. I am not saying that there is no place in our dealings one with another for what may be learned thanks to counselling, psychotherapy techniques and holistic approaches to therapy (increasingly other churches - or others' churches - are doing the same). I am not saying that the learning of meditative techniques, from the monastic traditions of any one of a number of religions, is beyond the pale. It is meditation, of course. And though it may indeed have an important 'centering' function, it is not worship. In the context of a Meeting it is individualistic, shutting out the others who are hoping to be 'gathered' (as does reading through Meeting). In fact I am showing solidarity with several recent Swarthmore lecturers.

Just as it was important for Chris Cook and Brenda Heales (1992), so it matters for me that Quakerism should not become enslaved, conformed to, elements chosen from the emporium of religions and world-views - including the world-view of the counsellor, the social-worker, the psychologist or the sociologist (and some of my best friends and Friends...), any more than it wanted to be in hock to the theologian. They wrote of the increasing emergence of 'Meeting for Counselling', 'Meeting for Case-Conference' and 'Meeting for Discussion', with worship being relegated to the sidelines, if not absent. God was scarcely getting a word in.

I think, too, that Margaret Heathfield (1994) was right to pose her question, and that it is one we should not shirk. Do we, or do we not, want to be 'a people of God' rather than an 'open spiritual movement'? 'We may not be able to continue indefinitely to keep all our options open', she warned. We may be forced to choose.[15]

Finally in this catalogue of solidarity, and with that optimism for which Friends are famed, I think that Jonathan Dale (1996) was right, and that we can rediscover that 'we were a people with a call'. For like him I too believe that we

> cannot be contented with the individualistic and relativistic and fragmentary Quakerism of this time. It drifts on the times when the times are for resisting. It undermines our confidence in our coherence often without good foundation. It weakens our corporate life. Unchecked, it could destroy...[16]

Above all, as the end of the millennium approaches we must not allow to become reality the (doomsday?) 'scenario' which Ben Pink Dandelion presented in discussing Implications. It is one I would also characterise as a special danger deriving from niche marketing - advertising our wares as of special interest for universalists or crypto-Buddhists, unitarian Christians or whatever, without due holistic care for the what and why of Quakerism. What Dandelion pointed to was the Religious Society of Friends becoming a collection of method-oriented groups in schism: individualism pushed beyond denominational bounds into the 'anarchist extreme' of sectarianism.[17]

Acts of defiance

The present Chief Rabbi has observed that our culture has moved so far from its religious roots 'that it now takes almost an act of defiance to use words like revelation, truth and authority in their traditional sense'.[18]

- We must not lose acts of defiance. Of all people Quakers have been associated with them, transforming as they did the 'traditional', and making of revelation and truth things experienced personally and inwardly (as well as corporately), for the guidance of the individual and the group.

- We need defiant declaration of things we know to be inalienable truths - those things which have formed and informed our very being as a Society and its actions, and which have the power still to do so. If we have among us people who doubt the existence of such things, who think that we have rightly abandoned expectation of such things, who do not know what they are, or if we can not agree on them, then that is a measure of the Society's problem. It needs to address it.

- We must not fear to reclaim a language of conviction. Without it we risk swelling the ranks of the snake oil salesmen and pedlars of feel-good spirituality which are abundant in our world as the 21st century draws near.

• We must not allow tentativeness to replace Truth (once we have decided what it is - and if it ever existed, which some of us doubt). We must not be seduced away from order and tradition or despise profession. For when George Fox criticised 'professors' of religion it was not the fact of their professing that he despised, but rather the falsity of it, divorced from the transforming experience and the making of truths one's own.

• In like vein, pontificating is a proper undertaking for Friends. This word, after all, speaks of bridge-making, being a means of access and progress for 'the things that are eternal' and perhaps, too, given the diversity which modern Quakerism represents, for the joining of divergencies without falling into the fudge and sludge beneath.

• On each side of the bank are others who are looking for a way to join hands, and our pontificating might help them. That is proselytising - a bringing over (and it is as well to remember that the proselyte was one who wanted to come). Professing, pontificating[19] and proselytising are proper roles for Quakers.

• And we must evangelise - though that word strikes horror into the breasts of Friends. The word 'outreach', favoured by Quakers, I find mealy-mouthed. It speaks to me of a tentativeness of outstretched arm which should be accompanied by an 'if it's alright with you' or 'would you just mind if ...' (like the well-worn joke that reads 'the meek shall inherit the earth ... if that's alright with the rest of you'). To spread good news (evangelise) is a right and proper thing to do, if we believe that Quakerism carries good news and is worth knowing.

If we do not think so, then indeed why are we ?

Previous Convictions

PART TWO

faith, values
and their
transmission

chapter eight

FAITH AND THE FAITH

AITH, THE FAITH, keeping faith, keeping the faith, faithfulness ... this is the language of belief and commitment, of trust and hanging on. Our Book of Discipline is a book of Faith and Practice. The latter - the doing of things Quakerly - is a product of the former and is not a substitute for it.

It is a great temptation to define the faith of Friends, when we are asked, in terms of what we are not and what we do not do (such as have clergy or celebrate sacraments). In fact we do ... though in ways more radically defined than in most Christian traditions. Our priesthood is extensive and it is required of each one of us. Our sacramentalism, we are taught, should pervade the whole of life and practice. And as for faith as trust and reliance (which is an important New Testament meaning of the word, though not the only meaning in that source), arguably Friends need it more than most, for neither do we depend on the mediating power of Church, sacraments and specially-trained priesthood nor do we hold to the idea that an agreed corpus of words mediated by Tradition, and carrying assurances and affirmations of faith, will carry weight.

I have always thought (and despite the counter-assurances of BAPSOC and the Christian Union in my university days) that our individual agnosticism carries with it a largely unrecognised helping of faith. Though as yet I do not know - on lots of fronts - yet I act in trust that what is needed will be given me, while I hold fast to what I have known and continue to look for authentic signs of God's presence. It has never been my experience that faith or the faith has come to me in a complete package.

The Book of Discipline (ie a record of, and guide for, our discipleship) tells us at the outset: 'We must trust that faith is robust, compassionate and "not quick to take offence"' (p 13), for in the absence of a creed and a liturgy we do not have a body of language to which all must, or can assent, and there will be a variety of expressions of faith among us. Its robustness depends on our individual and corporate relationship with That which is the object of faith. Using Christian language of a traditional kind we might say that knowing the Lord of the work does indeed bear fruit in doing the work of the Lord.

The faith, by contrast, is that which makes us Quakers rather than anything else. It is the testimonies and traditions which have sprung from, and coloured our understanding of, God and Christ, humankind and our world. For me it is the Quaker understanding of Christianity.

Answering back and hanging on

Much of what is written about faith concerns the difficulty of holding on to it at times. Many of the religious jokes are about this too, and about our self-deceptions, half-heartedness, routine or forgotten observances, bargaining and insurance-policy approach to walking with God. Jewish jokes are the best, and Jewish literature is more argument than finality, more debate than dogma, more casuistry ('what if ...') than creed. I don't find it hard to identify with the Jewish joke, which is very often less a joke than a teaching tool.

Jewish Joke 1

A woman watches in despair as her only son is swept out to sea. 'G-d of Abraham, Isaac and Jacob', she cries, 'would you take my son from me? I who have kept kosher, some of the time, and have kindled the Sabbath lights? I will serve You with my whole heart if You will return him to me!' At that moment a great wave swept on to the shore, depositing the child unharmed. The woman looked heavenward and after a pause said 'There was a hat ...?'

Jewish Joke 2

A man falls over a cliff. His fall is broken by a small branch to which he clings perilously, sure to tumble. He calls desperately, 'Help, help, is there anybody there?' A voice comes from Heaven. 'Let go - my arms are beneath you.' There was a pause. 'Is there anybody else there?'

Jewish Joke 3

A non-observant Jew went on holiday to Egypt where, following the Camp David Accord and as a gesture of solidarity, the camels had been taught to respond to commands in Hebrew. To make the camel go, the rider uttered a blessing on the Name of G-d (Baruch ha'Shem). To stop, the camel responded to the beginning of a very familiar piece of liturgy, 'Hear, O Israel...' (Shema^e Yisrael). The camel set off to Baruch ha'Shem, but getting carried away was heading at speed towards the - inevitable - precipice. The rider had forgotten the command for 'stop', but being Jewish (albeit non-observant), at the moment of imminent death he uttered 'Shema^e Yisrael'. The camel stopped. In relief he shouted 'Baruch ha'Shem.'

As we transmit what we understand by faith and as we illustrate the ways in which (in our experience and in that of others) it is encountered or lost, jeopardised, held fast, bolstered, built up and victorious against the odds, we must not fail to record the wrestling with God and the anger, the bleakness as well as the moments of insight and joy, and the fun.

'Held' in the faith

Most of the men in my family had worked at the coal face - in the days when there were deep coal mines in Wales. My grandfather, by contrast, for many years operated and maintained a haulage engine underground, while my father was a blacksmith on the surface of a coal mine. The exception to this unexceptional male history was maternal grandfather's own uncle. In the early decades of this century uncle Jacob had been the Mines Agent.

This was a boss's job, and his was a very grand house, a presence at civic occasions and a substantial marble memorial in the cemetery at Aberdare. It was this last which created the family ill-feeling.

In uncle Jacob's generation the family (on my mother's side) was still chapel-going, though split between the English and the Welsh Baptists. Uncle Jacob was in the Welsh half of the divide. Around three of the four sides of the marble memorial cube were the words of 2 Timothy 4:7 -

Mi a ymdrechais ymdrech dêg
Mi a orphenais fy ngyrfa
Mi a gedwais y ffydd.

Like the writer of 2 Timothy, uncle Jacob was saying that he had fought a good (spiritual) fight, had run the race of life and had kept the faith (cf Galatians 1:23). The first two, the family thought, were uncontroversial. The third

... well anyone would have had some nerve to claim such a thing!

It was the faith that uncle Jacob and the author of 1 Timothy were talking about. It was a body of teaching acknowledged as authoritative, to which they assented. They preserved ('kept') and also transmitted it. More often for Paul[1] the word faith signified reliance. That reliance was in what God was, what God had done through Jesus Christ and had promised for you. No more was demanded. All else followed from this faith. So it would have been less controversial (as my family saw it) for uncle Jacob to have said that he had been a man of faithfulness and a man who trusted in God. But 'keeping the faith' sounded to them altogether too credal and 'Catholic', as well as open to doubt so far as his history was concerned!

So faith/ffydd was an important word in my own chapel-going days. Faith was what kept you in the pews. Faith was what got you into the waters of full-immersion baptism. No infant could show it. No young person below the age of discernment could lay claim to it so as to be baptised. Baptism was for adult believers. It was an individual matter, though of course it was in a community of faith that the path to faith was smoothed. The faith came a poor second.

But late in 1996 I was in a conference of Jews and Christians considering the theme of covenant. Mostly oblivious of the fact that here were two religions divided by much of the same vocabulary (for both sides were not always using the same words in the same way), there was much Christian talk of covenantal belonging and commitment and the inheritance from Abraham. There was a lot of talk about the need for Christians to make public commitment - for covenant signifies agreement to, and thereafter binds one in a relationship of belonging.

In the chair was a professor of Theology who is also a Methodist minister. Very quietly she said that she was glad she came from a tradition in which her son, now more than thirty years old and severely handicapped mentally and physically, could be 'held' before God and taken fully into the faith community, without asking of him any personal statement of faith or commitment at all.

We know that there is a place for this. And such moving (and extreme) examples apart, there is something to be said for 'holding' as a community those of us whose understanding and commitment is, for whatever reason, imperfect. The Religious Society of Friends has been able to do this. There is a lot to be said for not demanding a statement which must conform to 'the faith', in immutable fashion. And the Religious Society of Friends is like that.

But there is nothing to be said, in my view, for avoiding questions of faith, the faith and faithfulness/commitment amongst ourselves, as if claimed association with the group were sufficient and the end of the matter. There is nothing to be said for treating seeking and less than wholehearted faith/faithfulness as more important than finding, as if our purpose should not be to promote growth in faith, commitment and understanding. To that end we need, as Quakers, to transmit what we know of faith.

Receiving and delivering

Some stories stand the test of time. They have been passed from generation to generation in a line of 'witnesses' and the very fact of such passing imbues them with a status which other stories do not have. In some religious groups the fact of the passing on, and the identity of the transmitters matters a lot ('Rabbi X received from Rabbi Y', or the lines for transmission of Hadith in Islam, for example). It was important to be able to trace a teaching to a reliable source, preferably to the founder of the faith itself.

In the New Testament Paul sometimes had to defend his position as an apostle and as a teacher. He appealed to his sense of 'calling' and the fact that he was no less an eyewitness of the resurrected Jesus Christ than other 'pillars' of the Christian community were. He appealed to the fact that he (like other Christians) was a charismatic - imbued with the Spirit, gifted with the power of discernment ('and I think I have the Spirit of God'). And also he appealed to the fact that he taught what others taught - that is, he knew the 'received' tradition and faithfully had transmitted it. His insights were also testable against a wider whole. While personal experience and the benefit of spiritual discernment were very important, these did not override the need for teaching which could not be dismissed as merely individualistic.

Not surprisingly the words 'receive' and 'deliver' recur in his writings: 'For I received from the Lord what I also delivered to you, that the Lord Jesus on the night he was betrayed took bread ...' (1 Corinthians 11:23). Or this:

> I preached to you the Gospel which you received ... I delivered to you, as being of the first importance that which I also received, that Christ died for our sins in accordance with the Scriptures, that he was buried, that he was raised on the third day... and that he appeared to Cephas then to the twelve ... Last of all ... he appeared also to me.
>
> (1 Corinthians 15: 1-5 cf Romans 6:17; Galatians 1:9-23; 1 Thessalonians 2:13)

In the latter case the certainty which came of personal experience was combined with knowledge of a tradition, which told of the related, but distinctive, experiences of others. On this basis Paul passed on the news.

Faith had come out of an experience of encounter. Knowledge was incomplete (1 Corinthians 13), but enough *was known to make that 'leap of faith' which meant that ever after, Paul's hand was (metaphorically speaking) in the hand of God and he was 'going along with' the journey, in trust of its end. 'Faith is the assurance of things hoped for, the conviction of things not seen', wrote the author of the Letter to the Hebrews (11:1), thereafter itemising a line of witnesses to such leaps of faith.*

As for the faith, Paul did not assume that you could interweave your life story with that of someone else unless you knew their story:

> *You were buried with him by baptism ... so that as Christ was raised from the dead ...we too might walk in newness of life...*
>
> Romans 6:4

Thus there was a corpus of traditional tales which needed to be passed on, for how else would you know what the standards now were, and what had happened to cause the standards to be altered so radically? What was received was thereafter delivered. Teaching about faith and values was transmitted.

'Quaker faith and ...'

Our book of discipline, Quaker Faith and Practice, preserves for us both senses of faith and the faith. Within the pages of Quaker Faith and Practice there are plenty of incidences of faith in the sense of a trusting walk with the beloved, a communion of understanding which can ride adversity and a certainty that the Other is trustworthy.

As for the faith, for more than three centuries there have been things that Friends needed to know if they were identifiably to be, and to act as, Friends. And clerks, elders and the like, needed some point of reference, apart from their own 'sense' of a matter, in decision making. The precursors of our modern books of discipline (as Quaker

Faith and Practice pp 13 and 613 explain) were divided into doctrine, practice and church government. 'Doctrine' disappeared as a title post 1921, replaced by 'Christian life, faith and thought'. The faith is there too.

Friends' non-credalism does not mean that they have no body of tradition to which to look. Quakerism's Testimonies (like tradition subject to re-appraisal generation by generation) stand as a canon, ie a measure, against which individual Quaker faith and practice is assessed.

But these things are of little value to us if they are not known, and if we do not ask of incomers and members of long standing that they understand them.[2]

* * *

The poet Waldo Williams was right, of course (as quoted and translated in Quaker Faith & Practice, 26.64):

> Yn y pen draw nid oes gan un a dderbynio'r grefydd fwyaf traddodiadol ddim ond ei brofiad i bwyso arno

translated as:

> In the end, even the one who accepts the most traditional religion has nothing but his own experience to rely on.

But he was right on other occasions too, as in the poem Preseli where he ended with the expression cadw y ffynon rhag y baw. We need to ensure a purity of transmission, without adding to or taking away from what has been given. It is we who may be channels for the experience which others enjoy. We must ensure that the living water can flow freely from its source and that things about us do not impede it. So as Waldo said, we must see that we 'keep the well-spring free of muck'.

chapter nine

FAMILY VALUES

I am the family face;
Flesh perishes, I live on,
Projecting trait and trace
Through time to times anon
And leaping from place to place
over oblivion

Moments of Vision
Thomas Hardy

FAITH AND VALUES ARE transmitted in community. In Part One of *Previous Convictions* I wrote about my own perceptions of late twentieth century Quakerism, expressing my concern that we may be experiencing an erosion of a sense of Quaker community. This may be due to increased individualism and due also to diminished knowledge of (and interest in) our testimonies and tradition and in those values which in the past have characterised Friends. With such an erosion there may come less of an ability to act or to speak corporately, as a people of God, as well as less financial support for what is done in our name.

When the Siddur posed all those What? questions ('What are we? etc), however, it also offered some clues as to answers. The synagogue liturgy had gone on 'We are a people ... let us create ...' Just as God in that liturgy withdrew from divine domination, so the Christ of John's Gospel (14:15) laid aside a relation of domination and said 'I do not call you servants, for the servant does not

know what his master is doing. I have called you friends.'
To his friends (according to that Gospel), and with a
directness which we celebrate as Friends, there was given
a promise that teaching, such as there was already, would
not be cut short. It would continue through the Spirit's
leadings, 'into all truth'. From the outset of Quakerism,
Friends believed that this matched their own experience
as a group, as well as personally.

The family hearth

It is the community, over time, which determines what
manifestations of Truth, of the faith, and what values
are characteristic of itself, or peculiar to itself. These may
change as generations pass. This community is comprised
of individuals in relationship one with another and I shall
consider the family model of community, because
Quakers, particularly those whose discovery of Quakerism
has come after a long period of 'belonging' nowhere, or
of seeking, often talk of 'coming home'.[1] Almost always
that sense of 'homecoming' had something to do with
experience of Friends' Meeting for worship.

We describe the Meeting for worship in a variety of
ways. It is the power-house of Quakerism; it is the heart
of the body; it is the hub of the wheel from which the
spokes of our activities emerge. It is (waxing romantic)
the warm hearth to which the family of Friends returns
and from which it gets up and goes forth to meet a colder
world, warmed for the task (were Quakers ever to
introduce liturgical 'words of dismissal', I imagine they
might be that recurring 17th century Friends' cry: 'Arise
and be doing !').

For Isaac Penington the gathered group was the fire
itself, with Quakers 'an heap of living coals warming one
another'.[2] Coals together release heat, light, energy.
Removed from their place in the hearth and laid out
individually they quickly lose their power. It comes as no

surprise to find that this is a truism beloved of writers on the Church.

It is in the family, the Meeting, that we are 'known' (or should be), however anonymous we are to much of the world outside. But to function well, the family must not stifle. To nurture people of maturity and lovingkindness it must not be inward-looking.

> A family which lives entirely for itself becomes not a family but a prison

wrote George Guiver, from the Anglican Community of the Resurrection at Mirfield. Though conversely

> a family which lives entirely for other people cannot hope to remain a family either: its 'family-ness' will ultimately be dissipated.[3]

It is the balance of these things which Meetings have to preserve. They need the nurture which builds up and provides, in turn, that store of spiritual energy which makes possible the living 'for other people'.

'The gospel', George Guiver went on, 'does not sit happily with a body which contains within itself enduring conflicts of interest' (and he was addressing primarily an Anglican audience, I think). No more can good news be spread when the spiritual life of the messengers is impoverished. There is little nourishment from

> a Church starved of commerce with the Beloved, which, when asked to describe him, is embarrassed and stuck for something to say.[4]

This chapter is about what families find to say and about the fact that loving acts come most from families which know the experience of love.

The story-telling family

We take from a family - if it is not dysfunctional - security and its acceptance of our strengths and weaknesses, joys and sorrow. It is there that we learn first that there can not be an answer for everything but that there is also the matter of living with the questions. It is there that we discover moral education, not just in terms of guidance about choices but as becoming part of community in microcosm. We expect that we will be censured for letting it down. We bear its name and carry with us its values when we are beyond its confines. We may jeopardise its reputation.

The word linked with family is home rather than hotel, though it's a common complaint of parents that their children treat it like one! We may sometimes resent our obligations to family, we may not necessarily like everyone in it to the same degree. We may have to struggle with actual dislike of some. But it is a moral community, a place where values are transmitted (if we are fortunate they are good ones), a source of identity. It is there that the rites of passage are marked. So it may be with Meetings too.

The family is also a narrative institution - snapshots are shared - where stories of the past are told and where we tell our own. We discover who from the past we most resemble and whose story we can least identify with.

I admit I was always rather impressed by the tale of my formidable great-grandmother, fresh from the wet-fish merchant, who once struck her contentious next door neighbour with a large haddock. Remembering her penchant for gifting uncomfortable (but good Welsh) flannel underwear to my six year old self, I believed she was capable of it. I told the story on a Radio Wales 'God-slot' just before Jewish New Year in 1996, to receive a number of letters telling similar piscatorial tales - some from members of the Jewish community in South Wales.

Repentance is in the air at Rosh ha Shanah !⁵ I know I have things in common with my great-grandmother.

The story-telling family, then, is the storehouse of collective memory, whether we come to it by birth, marriage or adoption. It is where visions and hopes for the future emerge. Those among us who were born into Quaker families, and/or have grown into family allegiance through a Quaker school, also understand the language of family in terms of real blood ties, the experiences of growing up, and by being a link in a chain which may go back many generations. For most Friends nowadays, it is a matter of adoption.⁶

However the family of Friends in our Meeting is made up, it is reliant on individuals to tell the tales. A community

> has no tradition, no common memory, apart from persons who open their hearts to make public what is in them

as Haddon Wilmer has written.⁷ The analogy holds good for our Meetings too, I think.

Our family/community is being created anew, not from nothing but with elements of the old, in each generation. The early Friends' use of the language of spiritual birthing may remind us that we can have a role in the spiritual parenting of one another. Friends in their Meetings are midwives, if not always actual mothers and fathers, to the next generation of Friends being created, for the Spirit works through individuals and Meetings.

'We are a people ... let us create ...' In the absence of paid priesthood, it is our call to be 'father' and 'mother' to one another, in coming into fullness of being, as well as to be brother, sister and Friend. Ours is a family in which we may be called to many roles.

The family history

'Having come home, we should know our family history,' said Margaret Hope Bacon, American historian of Quakerism, in a conference on Quaker Foremothers in Woodbrooke in 1994. Many of us do not, and know of no reason why we should be interested in it or feel connected with the past of Quakerism. In fact as Alastair Heron found, it is right to speak of 'the patchy knowledge about "the Quaker heritage" displayed by many Quakers throughout Britain'.[8]

The paradox is that as the barriers which obscure the past have been pushed back as never before - as we have the chance to know more of our own group's history, of human history and of that of the universe, so too, it would seem, has our identification with that past declined. Connectedness is not a contemporary ideal. It is no wonder that Grace Davie's study of religion in Britain at this time is subtitled Believing without Belonging.[9]

Yet it is disempowering not to know a history or to be deprived of it. Many a woman in the world of Islam has come to know that. For we may be left in ignorance of the wealth of options, freedoms, challenges and opportunities which are ours by inheritance, if only we knew of them. And we know nothing of the 'depth of the teaching' which our tradition has had to offer. In families we learn. Families have an obligation to teach.

Not a hotel

We are used to the idea of the hotel as a retreat for convenience, quiet, personal satisfaction and a point from which we shall at some time move on. There is no cause to think of a hotel in terms of family. We need not concern ourselves much with the collective welfare of our fellow guests or offer to work for the improvement of the hotel. The transaction is an individual one. Meetings, and the

Religious Society of Friends, by contrast, need to promote the family paradigm and to create a setting in which we are truly 'at home' to callers. We should not be 'guests ourselves, wanting other people to take on the responsibilities of the host' [10] - or to put matters another way - Meister Eckhart's way, allow them to find that:

God is at home,
It is we who have gone out for a walk.

We should allow, of course, that some in our circle will move out and move on. We should wonder why it is that some who have chosen to live and work with us for a long time nevertheless do not feel that they want to marry themselves to the family name. The phenomenon of long-term attendance, without membership, increases. [11] The challenge for Friends is to create that sense of connectedness which cuts across tenuous association and a holding back from the final step of membership.

The Family Abroad

There is more to a family than what a few sets of walls enclose. There are other Quaker family members 'out there', in other Meetings, here and overseas. We are bound to them by ties of kinship and a common name, though in some ways they may be quite unlike us. World-wide Quakerism is varied in its forms. In our Meetings we need opportunities to know the collective history and to discover who we most resemble, admire or identify with. British Quakerism, though first on the world-wide scene, is in many respects untypical.

After the first International Conference of Quaker Women, held at Woodbrooke in 1990, there were visits to Swarthmoor Hall and to Lancaster Castle, scene of imprisonment for many seventeenth century Friends. The Hall, Janet Scott reported, gave a sense of family and shared ancestry to this international, polyglot group of visitors. Lancaster Castle struck other chords, however – such as most British Friends, thankfully, have long ceased hearing in their nightmares.

> We had been through rooms which held fetters and instruments of torture. We had seen the dark, crowded cells. For some of us, this was too much. For among us were those for whom this is not history but a present, everyday reality.[12]

Some of the family knows about living in a hostile environment, where relativism, doubt as a virtue, pleading perplexity and the perpetual Quaker question-mark have no place.

***

Having 'come home', we need to know our family history. Whether our personal relation to the past and to other forms of Quakerism is one of attraction or repulsion, rejection or a sense of loss; whether we go in for iconoclasm or flattering hagiography; whether we think in terms of continuity or the need to create something utterly different from what went before, still we need to know our history and tradition. It is the creator of whatever it is that we love, deplore or challenge in the Quakerism we have embraced.

'Keeping house in a cloud of witnesses'

Waldo Williams (1904-1971) was a fine 20th century poet of the Welsh language. He was also a Friend, having formerly been a Baptist. His poem *Mewn Dau Gae* ('In two fields') appears in *Quaker Faith and Practice*, the first such item in Welsh to figure in a Book of Discipline. In one of his poems, *Beth yw Byd?*, he posed the questions 'What is being a nation? What is love of country?' (Beth *yw bod yn genedl? ... Beth yw gwladgarwch?*). His answer, I think, could apply to love of anything which demands of us an understanding of what we are, a recognition that we as individuals are not the measure of all things and an answerability to our heritage.

These things, said Waldo, were to do with the deep things of the heart. Love of country was 'keeping house in a cloud of witnesses' (*cadw ty mewn cwmwl tystion*).[13]

Waldo was a man familiar with the language of the Bible. The New Testament's 'cloud of witnesses', in Hebrews 12:1, had referred back to chapter eleven, where readers were reminded of all those who had gone before them. Now (12:1-2) it was their turn, as Christians, to 'run the race', sensible of the 'cloud of witnesses' into which their forebears had been enveloped.

I like Waldo's analogy. I like the idea that my Quakerism is part of a continuum and that how I act and respond may be informed by the experience of those who have run the race, kept the house, before me (what else is Quaker Faith and Practice for?). I am even heartened, rather than threatened, by the idea of watchers and witnesses, whose previous convictions and invisible presence may sometimes bear silent witness against me, as well as for me when I do right - though this is not something I treat literally.

Truths and stories

The stories which families tell are not necessarily accurate, of course. There are half remembered things, things embellished by the generations of re-telling. Was it really a large haddock, or a haddock at all? Later versions speak more kindly of the family than did the original event. But that is par for the course. Someone (I forget who) once observed that a nation was a group united in a misconception about its own beginnings. Families harbour similar misconceptions, as do religious groups. Sometimes they are necessary for their survival and sanity, though it is as well that the self-deception is pointed out from time to time.

It may well be, for example, that the 'sword of William Penn' tale has no basis in history,[14] but it is important, nevertheless, that it continues to be told. For the family has recognised in it a truth about itself and its experience. Some of modern Friends' most cherished quotations (or 'catchphrases') - such as 'walk cheerfully over the world meeting that of God in every one', or the Balby Elders' disclaimer that 'these things we do not lay upon you as a rule ...' have now been torn from their original, religiously and morally challenging, and usually forgotten contexts, leaving us with things that are in danger of becoming cheery aphorisms. I am not happy about that, sterilising as it does the language which in some cases was that of more discomforting, challenging, biblically-based utterances. But this is not unusual either.

By contrast, however, the despising of history makes us prisoners of the present, unable or unwilling to unlock those treasures old, as well as new, which (like the head of a family does in his storeroom) the wise teacher brings forth for instruction and interpretation (Matthew 13:52). Certainly we do not abandon the house because some of those who lived in it were less saintly than many have liked to imagine. Nor is it helpful to suggest (building an analogy on David Boulton's 'cobbled together' Truth)[15] that there never was a house worth speaking of at all.

Part of the task of transmitting faith and values within Quakerism is to encourage understanding of the family's history and its stories.

'Your people will be my people'

The idea of being a people was important for the first Friends of Truth. The family was a powerful ideal too. They had, many of them, left their own families, or had been driven ignominiously from them. They were persecuted and derided. In some cases it was their blood relatives who had got them held in the stocks, who had tried to get them gaoled, had disinherited them and called their children bastards. Secretly, and at a later stage, those same relatives might venture at night to exhume the body of their lost loved one from the unconsecrated ground where Friends had buried it, so as to return it to the circle of the original family's dead. In the intervening years, however, it was the circle of Friends themselves which had provided the family for that person.

Quakers were their source of support, love and nurture. It was they who bound the wounds, brought food to the imprisoned and provided shoes for the feet of the travelling publishers of Truth and for other impoverished Friends. Sectarianism has always divided families. Think of the sects and cults you would least like to see your loved-one involved with - the politically dubious or revolutionary, the manipulative, those promoting change of personality or a cult of personality, the doomsday kind, or some other. Quakerism seemed, perhaps was, all of these at one moment or another in its early history.[16] Hence the high level of public disquiet about Quakerism in the 1650's and 60's. Had you ventured into it, allied yourself with this new family, you would probably then have looked to it as a haven of support in a hostile world. Who needed membership? Your incarceration, your financial ruin, and suffering the many penalties of non-conformity - these were proof positive of which family you belonged to.

The first 'convincements' to Quakerism brought an about turn as radical as that of the biblical Ruth when she made her commitment to her mother-in-law Naomi. That had been termed in the simplest of language, but it was profound:

> your people will be my people, and your God my God.

Ruth 1:16

Certainly the God which the first Friends embraced was not different (the one Ruth now worshipped was, of course), but in terms of the understanding of that God, and the response required, there had been change indeed.

Those who were 'convinced' as Friends of Truth were now part of a prophetic society, in the vanguard of change, or so they believed. So it is not surprising that quite a few in the seventeenth century waxed over-enthusiastic about some of the movement's leading figures, George Fox and Margaret Fell in particular. They praised them lavishly, excessively, for their spiritual parenting, just as some felt strong and emotional loyalties to James Nayler, or John Perrot and the like.

Nor is it surprising to find references to 'the motherly woman' in Friends' letters and Minutes. This female Friend who brought you food in prison, or fed, encouraged and comforted your children in their makeshift schoolrooms after their battle through the streets against sticks and stones, was no aproned Martha in the private domain. She was probably an embattled public preacher in her own right or a prophetess in opposition to the authorities. But in addition, her bread, broth and beer were true sustenance in what was now the best family you had.[17]

***

The early Friends' situation forged a sense of identity, of familial solidarity and mutual up-building. They knew who they were (after some initial confusion, and concentration on all things being lawful while forgetting that some were not expedient). They were a people of God, a nation of priests.

A century and more later, things had changed. Inward rather than outward-looking, a family not least because of the degree of inter-marriage within it, Quakerism had become a system of kinship in which marriages were determined (in the 'better' Quaker circles, at least) as much with a view to social and business connections as to excellence of 'conversation'.

In our own century Quakerism is no longer the kind of sect which requires endogamous marriage, nor is it bound together by the bonds of persecution. We are no longer as Friends (in Britain at least) challenged by dire circumstances to make public in what our faith rests and what we would die for (would there be enough evidence to convict us?). What we would die for is not a matter which the Advices and Queries address, though such a challenge must concentrate the mind wonderfully, again shifting the emphasis from that perennial Quaker question mark to the exclamation mark.

But the need for familial solidarity, understanding and unity of purpose remains.

Saying 'we' ...

Rabbi friends of mine tell me that they grow tired of having to disabuse non-Jewish enthusiasts for the wonders of Jewish family life. In reality, they say, Jewish family life is little better or worse than anyone else's family life. Judaism, of course, does carry as central to itself an emphasis on community and solidarity, bolstered by a willingness to identify with the history and experiences of the group. This, one might expect, is a foil to some of the tendencies of late twentieth century individualism, though it proves to be no guarantee of any such thing, of course. And so the warnings come: 'The contradiction at the heart of individualism', wrote the present Chief Rabbi, addressing his own community as well as the rest of us,

> is that there can be a self unencumbered by tradition, unfettered in its freedom ... a kingdom without a country.[18]

Judaism stresses belonging, including the obligations which go with it. As my Reform Rabbi Friend told me when she was speaking of induction, 'there comes a point when they start to say "we"'.[19]

The same thing emerged when Harvey Gillman reviewed (the liberal Jewish) Rabbi Julia Neuberger's book On Being Jewish in The Friend (April 5th 1996). He noted that certain things in it were appropriate to Friends. It asked the question 'How far can a tradition go and still maintain that it is faithful to its sources?'[20] Liberal Judaism, he pointed out, like Quakerism emphasised continuous revelation, had links with the peace movement, strong social concerns, openness to newcomers and equality of men and women. 'But it also has something which Friends might envy', he went on. That was a strong sense of community. In the case of Judaism this was linked with consciousness of being a minority, against the background of a common history and shared persecution.

Judaism (even the most liberal in speaking of continuous revelation) carries an assumption of continuity. So for every Jew, regardless of whether s/he is a recent convert, is involved only peripherally in the practice of the religion, or ultra-orthodox, it is taken to be true that 'A wandering Aramean was my father ...' (Deuteronomy 25:5-9), just as for every Jew gathered for a Passover Seder it is as if s/he too had emerged from bondage in Egypt. All stand again in spirit at the foot of Mt Sinai.

It is not only Jews who find such language of identification powerful, and who are challenged by their own association with a long heritage of faith and spiritual struggle. I am one who values the 'cloud of witnesses'.

Nevertheless, those who preach continuity are sometimes accused of advocating living in the past. Those who speak of remaining true to a history are thought to be suffering entrapment in history. I do not believe that the past is as holy as the present. But in any case, the Quaker past, and the varieties of Quaker witnesses, are great enough to embrace many people. We still have (as Margaret Heathfield wrote in her 1994 Swarthmore Lecture *Being Together*) 'modern day representatives of almost every phase of our history … as a more or less complete fossil record of our Quaker past'. Feeling oneself in a line of continuity is a useful foil to ultra-individualism, I think.

On the fringe of the family

The researchers, and Friends travelling under Concern, are suggesting that there has been some erosion of the sense of Quaker community. With this comes decreased commitment to the Society and its work. In part this may be due to increased loyalty to the local Meeting or due perhaps to a different perception of 'home', which locates it in one of the 'special interest' groups associated with Friends.[21]

> Religious Humanists, Quaker Unitarians, Christian Universalists, positive agnostics will feel at home in the Quaker Universalist Group. [emphasis mine]

reads the advertisement which has appeared regularly in The Friend.

Many of the members of QUG, it should be said (as of the members of Q-ROOM, the Friends Homosexual Fellowship etc), also have a firm loyalty to the wider Society and its work. But we need to regard it as our own failure that some Friends find special interest groups more obviously their 'home' than the Religious Society of Friends itself.[22]

The 'we' of Quakerism has to be broader than that which a special interest group embraces. Similarly the 'we' of now is part of a bigger we which embraces past and future generations. So whether we are by birth or adoption in the family, the family's stories should be known, so that our own may be integrated fully with them, to make sense of an increasingly confused present. We need to teach and to initiate teaching, rather than to wait for sometimes reticent or uncertain enquirers and attenders to make the running.[23]

The memory of which I write is not the kind of which the historian is the custodian. Nor is it the collective memory associated with theories about the psyche and Jungian archetypes. It is to do with the work of the group:

> only the group can bequeath both language and transpersonal memory.[24]

That's what a family is for.

Two stories

The stories which follow are to do with a sense of belonging. Both of them relate to experiences I had in Israel.

Story 1

In May of 1995 I was visiting Israel with a group from the Council of Christians and Jews. There I met a Jerusalemite who is not yet middle-aged who has stayed in my memory. He was born and brought up in Mea Shearim, the teeming, ultra-orthodox section of the city, where the dress is that of the ghettoes of centuries ago, and where the pale faces of some of the men speak of long hours in ill-lit rooms in the study of Torah. I met him on several occasions in Jerusalem and in Tel Aviv and found him both impressive and disturbing of my sense of who I might be.

This man had had a great depth of traditional Jewish religious learning but little by way of secular education. In recent years he has made himself multi-lingual and well-versed in the kind of writing which is familiar enough to the educated western man. Of itself this is no mean feat. But he has taken this road at great price.

No longer is he part of Mea Shearim. No longer, in the 'outside' world, does he have a wife and children. He is still an observant, Orthodox Jew but now he acts as an interpreter of culture, explaining his former community and its concerns to those who need, or want, to know - to politicians, visiting delegations, tourists at the top end of the market. Those who once knew him well shout abuse in the streets. He looks at you very intently, and with eyes that seem sad, I thought.

On our last night in Israel our CCJ collective was entertaining itself after dinner in the hotel. He was with us. 'The Welsh can sing,' shouted a cheery bishop - 'Christine should sing us a song.' So I sang them a folk song in Welsh, all minor key and poignant, as these often are. He said to me later, 'We have songs like these.' And I was sad, because I didn't like to ask what the 'we' meant.

Story 2

'Keeping house in a cloud of witnesses' would surely have meaning for many Jews, who feel it is important to know where you belong. I felt that I had just a glimpse of the truth of this when I was visiting the Museum of the Diaspora in Tel Aviv. What follows need not apply to Jewishness and Judaism alone, I think.

The Museum of the Diaspora contains a Memorial Column. It is a remarkable piece of art which is in fact a kind of suspended, narrow cage, disappearing storeys-high into the heights of the building. To get the full effect you must decide to step (a little nervously in my case) beneath its suspended wrought metal bulk. Its shadow touches you.

Stepping under it you become part of it, one with the memories it represents. It is about self-identification. I was conscious that I was not a Jew, and that my memories could not be at one with theirs. As you stand beneath it, however, you are neither enclosed nor weighed down. You are not caged but free. You are acting in trust that its greatness will not destroy you. You become aware of the pattern created, of the distance it stretches from where you are, of it being so much bigger than you. You become aware that you, the 'something new', complete a pattern.

Once in your place, you can see the narrow but bright shaft of light which travels up through its heart from high above. You look into it and it embraces you too. Distance yourself only a little from the whole, and you do not see it for what it is.

Props and the family furniture

In the final paragraphs of this chapter I want to echo some of the themes of Previous Convictions and to speak of the importance of community/family as the framework within which our religious learning is done.

In her novel The Joy Luck Club Amy Tan begins as follows her chapter on Rose Hsu Jordan:

> As proof of her faith my mother used to carry a small leatherette Bible when she went to the First Chinese Baptist Church every Sunday. But later, after my mother lost her faith in God, that leatherette Bible wound up wedged under a too-short table-leg, a way for her to correct the imbalances of life ... my mother pretends that Bible isn't there ... But I know she sees it. My mother is not the best housekeeper in the world, and after all these years that Bible is still clean white.[25]

The woman's son had been drowned. Neither her will nor the faith on which she had been told to place such reliance could bring him back. Literally and metaphorically this Bible had acted as a prop, and now she claimed that she no longer saw a purpose for her faith. Others perceived a residue which was not without function. There was both preservation and rejection. 'Navigating through paradoxical, ambiguous territory' is what this is about.[26] And we do it all the time.

A Religious Society which sets great store by the 'What Canst Thou Say?' of present witness, which recognises the validity of (tested) present experience and which has found itself able to change a great deal over the few centuries of its existence may find itself able to identify with some of the things in the stories I use from time to time. It is important for us, as Friends, to be clear about which 'we' our allegiance is given to. We should consider, too, whether it is time for us to 'dust off' some of our previous convictions (and I am not talking about biblical certainties). It may be, even, that we have forgotten the extent to which they have been what has held the Society straight and steady.

'Which supports and challenges'

In 1993/4 Peggy Heeks was Joseph Rowntree Quaker Fellow. The report of her work as Fellow was published as Reaching to Community and she told of finding on her travels around Britain Yearly Meeting

> a longing for Quaker community, a community which is essentially Spirit-led, and which both supports and challenges.[27]

Sometimes it exists. In the 1994 anthology of Quaker family life compiled by Keith Redfern and Sue Collins, and called Relative Experience, E A Brown recorded falling away from Quakers in early adult life,

> only returning when I had my own children, appreciating the extended family of a Meeting that supported me in helping me define my view of Quaker parenting.

In that instance there was indeed the supportive ('extended family') community which was longed for and which challenged, so as to define and refine, and which promised nurture.

It, wrote Haddon Willmer, 'is a school of faith not least because it tests and challenges faith as well as rewards and encourages it'. It is where we are asked 'whether we have the courage and generosity to go on affirming the worth of human being in actual, present, deeply known persons'.[28] He might have been talking about a Friends' Meeting. In fact he was talking about the family.

chapter ten

THE MINISTRY OF TEACHING

MAINSTREAM CHRISTIAN churches assume that clergy and others will exercise a ministry of teaching and bishops have held in trust a responsibility for the soundness of the tradition transmitted. But ours is a 'do it yourself' religion, devolving responsibility onto each individual Friend, to whom the ultimate Teacher is accessible directly. So we have an obligation to teach one another and to learn.

Learning and spiritual nurture may go together, though not necessarily so. Not everything we learn will nurture us spiritually, but it is unlikely that we will be nurtured if we have no desire to learn.

'We are seekers ...'

'We are seekers but we are also holders of a precious heritage of discoveries' (Introduction to Quaker Faith and Practice, p 17). A great deal of teaching and learning does go on in the Society, and we have reason to be pleased about this. It goes on in study groups, through vocal ministry in Meetings and in special Meetings for Learning (in the USA such sessions sometimes precede Meeting for worship). It happens at residential weekends for that purpose or in 'one off' events, at attenders and enquirers' gatherings, through the provision of Meeting House libraries, in Monthly Meetings and General Meetings to which speakers are invited, in retreats and in one-to-one ministry (as for example through the work of Q-Room), through Woodbrooke programmes both in

Birmingham and 'on the road', through the publications which emerge from QHS, QSRE and QPS, and so on. Not least it goes on in our interactions one with another and in developing our understanding of, and relationship with, God.

Quaker Faith and Practice has a great deal to say about teaching and learning. It begins in the Advices and Queries with the Advice

> Take time to learn ... Remember the importance of the Bible, the writings of Friends and all writings which reveal the ways of God. (QFP 1.02 [5])

And it goes on (1.02 [16]) to speak of the need to 'increase your understanding' of the diversity of culture, language and expressions of faith in our Yearly Meeting and in the world community of Friends. There is more under such headings as education, teaching, elders, study and schools in its index and elders have a special responsibility in this sphere. 12. 12a of QFP tells of elders' job being

> to guide those who share in our meetings towards a deeper experience of worship; to encourage preparation of mind and spirit, and study of the bible and other writings that are spiritually helpful

and (12. 12e and h) they are to ensure that 'the basis and method of conducting meetings for church affairs are understood' and must encourage opportunities to broaden and deepen knowledge and understanding – about the roots and foundations of our faith, the insights of other faiths ... exploring how to deepen our ministry. They monitor the suitability of vocal ministry and should encourage it in others.

To guide, to encourage study, to ensure understanding and opportunities for learning and exploring, to broaden and deepen knowledge and to keep an eye on the appropriateness of behaviour and language is what a teacher does. Elders have a ministry of teaching. These things have been spelt out more clearly in the present Quaker Faith and Practice than was the case in Christian Faith and Practice (section 286). But it is not the work of elders alone.

'There were in the church of Antioch teachers'
(Acts 13:1)

My researches have often taken me in spirit to the early church of Antioch in Syria, where once Paul, Peter, Barnabas and other worthies from the apostolic age were to be found. There, before the age of bishops and before clerics claimed charism as their own and rendered it powerless in the hands of others, it was teachers and prophets whose knowledge and God-given insights were recognised as authoritative.[1] In earliest Christianity those appropriately gifted were commissioned (by God, they believed, and by the local church) to go out, teaching, prophesying and bearing witness. The first Friends of Truth understood this and prophecy and teaching/preaching were bases of the earliest Quaker activity.

In the unprogrammed and liberal tradition of British Friends we do not much favour formal instruction by individuals, or formalised preaching, or the theological training which takes place elsewhere in the world of Quakerism where they have paid ministers who need to be trained. We have more of the informal, with 'facilitating' of study and an open-ended approach. It is also, if we are honest, 'hit or miss'.

Provisions for teaching and learning vary considerably through BYM. And the charism of teaching takes on meaning here, for in some places it may well be down to a single enthusiast (a word meaning literally one in-spirit-ed), the charismatic organiser/teacher/facilitator, who encourages Friends into the ongoing learning and teaching process, who orders the book box from London, who seeks information from the Resources for Learning Network or scans the catalogues of study materials and produces the study pack as if from the magician's hat - and who ends up as leader. It may be an elder, it may not be.

The fact is that modern Quakers are not as good as we might expect (given that the Society includes so many teachers) at giving and accepting teaching and guidance.

> It has seemed strange to me that a Society with so many teachers in its midst is unable to explain itself to better advantage

was one observation recorded by Alastair Heron when studying the experience of new members.[2] As a result newcomers (or older hands) complain of receiving insufficient information about the Society, about its understanding of the Way, about membership and so on.[3] Statements about belief, in particular, are hard to prise from Friends, whether it concerns an individual's belief or where Quakerism stands on matters.[4] And there is also evidence about new kinds of reticence, such as did not exist in the age of our previous convictions. These too inhibit our teaching and learning.

Quenching the Spirit
(1 Thessalonians 5:19)

If some Friends are wary of taking on a teaching, or even a facilitating role at all, then why might this be? Perhaps believing that 'everything is partial and provisional' helps to account for it, 'so who am I to say anything?' Or it may be due to feeling that the teaching role is not egalitarian enough in a Quaker setting.[5] This kind of political correctness seems most odd in a group which for centuries has 'recognised' (as charismatic movements do) in individuals the gift of communication of experience and understanding.

In fact over the centuries Quakers have understood very well Paul's 'varieties of gifts but the same Spirit' (1 Corinthians 12:4). His list of the kinds of 'gifted' people who were needed (12:28) - apostles, prophets, teachers, administrators, healers - was re-manifested in the work of elders, recorded ministers, teachers in Friends' schools, publishers on Friends' behalf, overseers, clerks, missionary Friends, those with gifts of conciliation, counselling and healing, exhortatory ministers (preachers and prophets), Adult School teachers and so on, who were expected to teach and to nurture.

Doubt about the rightness of Quakers teaching others was unknown in the past. The doubts were about whether an individual felt truly 'led' to it or sufficiently equipped for it. This is surely a time when our world cries out for a ministry of teaching. It is not the time for the Religious Society of Friends to abandon one.

Secondly there are hesitations about learning as a group. Ben Pink Dandelion has itemised Friends' 'hesitations' about experience-based collective religious learning, and they give cause for concern, I think.[6] Notably there may be fear of 'speaking out' because the reality of diversity may be exposed and wounds opened. Sadly this 'self-censorship in speech acts'[7] and reliance on what is blissfully unsaid means that our testimony about plain speaking is breached as much among ourselves as outside of the group.

When hesitations like these also dribble into carefully-tailored, circumscribed ministry in Meeting for worship, or lead to lack of vocal ministry from many of us, then we have a recipe for a quenched Spirit, untaught, unnourished Meetings, starved of words of power.

Problems of the words and the Word

Our own personal knapsacks of spiritual resources which are precious to us probably contain a lot of words. Others may benefit from learning about them. Words are, after all (though often spoken of dismissively by Friends) the communication of community. In religious community the language of spiritual yearning and of finding should be shared.

Teaching and learning are achieved in many ways, of course, but often they involve words. Some Friends feel strongly that (so far as teaching is concerned) they do not have the words. They struggle to articulate, even for themselves, what it is of the things of the Spirit they know, do not know, have experienced or are seeking after. They find it hard to speak. Others may have many words, but fear that as yet the Word does not sufficiently inform them. There are some of us, too, who stay silent some of the time because of consciousness of having too many words.

Even I am reticent (some readers who know me will find this hard to believe!). I am always conscious that in many respects it's 'easy' for me. The language, the thought, the texts of religion are the air I breathe. They are my passion. I am paid to talk about them, argue about them, write about them, demand that they are examined in more than a superficial way. I know that I am in danger of rushing headlong down paths others might not wish to follow. Not all things are expedient.

But not all of us are so familiar with the language of religion or of faith, with the Bible generally and with other religious writings. We may be equally unfamiliar with the ways in which such things are understood and interpreted nowadays, despite the fact that for the last hundred years Friends have been encouraged to deal fearlessly with the Bible, for example, in the light of modern scholarship. This matter is important - that is of being aware of modes of interpretation, fresh perspectives and something of the history of how religious writings have been understood. Nowadays we are not working from the position in Fox's time, in which it could be assumed that the language of the Christian religion was very familiar indeed, but insufficiently internalised and enlivened by the Spirit in the experience of the believer.

There is a great challenge for our adult religious learning in this. Very often, in the 1990's, what we find is very superficial knowledge of such things, but plenty of prejudices about them, or a sense of hurt. If we propose to reject things as unhelpful to our own spiritual progress, it seems to me that at least we have an obligation to understand them, to help others understand why they seem troublesome and to inform ourselves sufficiently to be able to imagine their worth for other people. Just as the atheist may be asked to describe this God s/he doesn't believe in, and may discover that 'the believer' doesn't believe in that God either, so some may discover that Friends for whom the Bible, for example, is life and breath do not necessarily think of it, study it and rely on it in the ways they might assume.

It saddens me when I hear that study of Christianity and Bible study, in particular, are 'no go' areas for some Friends in some Meetings - as if Light from all quarters is to be welcomed, except from that which has illuminated Quakerism for over 300 years. I think of the story about another atheist, a famous and leading advocate of unbelief, who was once visited by a young admirer, eager to sit at the feet of this thinker. The young man was disturbed to discover at the house of his guru a library rich in books about religion. 'Why do you have all this stuff on religion?' he demanded. 'I am an atheist,' the philosopher replied. 'I am not an ignoramus.'

Faith beyond fear

It is important, then, that we help one another to reach beyond our fear and our reticence, whatever it may be about. Diversity is embraceable without fear in a group whose roots are securely grounded, where the identity of the whole is assured and understood and where each is certain that they do belong because they know, and at a deep level, what the shared truths are. Reticence and preferring to remain silent suggest a crisis of identity and fracturing community. They suggest that we have a lot to learn about ourselves, and a lot to teach each other. Fortunately we believe that we operate under the watchful care of a senior Teacher.

Perhaps we need to help each other reclaim a language of religious communication, a theological vocabulary and an understanding of the colourful patchwork of myth, parable, legend, poetry, biography, religious history, gospel and more. These things have told of humankind's experience on the religious quest. Some of it may inform our own. There are, in fact, plenty of aids to help us as adults in this process.

'There is no fear in love', wrote the author of 1 John 4:18, 'for perfect love casts out fear'. When we do show openness, share what we have been shown and learn together, then much of the time what we encounter is the surprise of recognition:

'others have known that too ... X is experiencing what I am ...

Y in the ancient past went the way that I am going

... haven't we all made that mistake? ...'

and the surprise of a new insight: 'I didn't know it said that' or 'is that what it means ...?'

This is exciting, reassuring and faith-promoting. And in the process of doing it, we may get beyond words.

'I delivered to you ...
that which I also received'
(1 Corinthians 15:3)

What we have received we must also deliver, after the manner of teachers and prophets. It will be about the faith, that is about our heritage and history, our testimonies, about the travellers' tales of pilgrims past, Quaker and otherwise, about the cloud of witnesses into which we in turn are enveloped.

It will include our own travellers' tales, that is it will also be about faith - the stories of God's dealing with us and our own response (and lack of), about our trustful waiting, our arguing and wrestling with God, our despair and our inability to believe. It will be about our encounters on the journey.

There are many Friends among us who know things that others need to know. They have those very 'words of power' which others of us are desperately in need of. Like true coin, such knowledge is unmistakable when we meet it. We will not meet it unless it is shared. And when it is shared, not only is there recognition, but also the realisation that the rest of us have been firing on half power.

***

In September 1996 I was in Paris attending a conference of historians of the early church. There a small number of opinionated Americans and Europeans worried over texts in a rarefied atmosphere. One of us was 'different', however.

From Ireland there had come an Irish-speaking Cistercian (Trappist) monk, quiet and weather-beaten from spending much of his time caring for cows. This man could dissect a Greek text with the best and gave what was left of his life, after prayer and cattle-keeping and the requirements of monastic obedience, to the study of early Christian literature and the writing of books about it.

Around the table historians of religion, Byzantinists, text critics and theologians opined about developments in the early Christian celibate and monastic traditions, and cited the Christian Fathers in support. But when he spoke, the rest of us shut up and listened. This was not just text or tradition. For him it was life and being. There were things that he knew which the rest of us did not, and we knew that he knew them. I think it was the difference, again, between the Life and knowledge of the lifestyle. The rest of us were engaged in karaoke.[8]

Speaking of faith ...

The early Quaker injunction about letting our lives preach (or 'speak' as we now tend to say) was not a signal that we should be silent in other ways. So I wonder whether it is a mark of our own uncertainty and a fear that we are not 'knowledgeable enough' which makes less than 40% of Quakers willing to identify themselves as such. Is this due to a conscious decision not to transmit news of Quakerism, or is it due, perhaps, to fear of being asked questions which we feel ill-equipped to answer?[9] The words light and bushel come to mind.

In my own place of work, I admit, I do not usually make any such announcements. Students of religion who demand challengingly of staff 'Are you a Buddhist/ Christian/Atheist?' have to be reminded that British universities operate no 'religious tests' (and would you demand of your politics tutor whether she voted Liberal Democrat?). But I don't hide clues. There are books about Quakerism on the shelves, a rather striking copy of a seventeenth century engraving called 'The Quakeress and the Devil' on my wall and a small teddy bear, dressed

George Fox style and carrying in his pocket a tiny, concertina-ed version of the Advices and Queries - but renamed Quaker Bearings. (Is the whirling sound I hear that of George Fox spinning in his grave?)

Had other people's Quakerism been less opaque, I think I might have been a Friend at an earlier stage. When I had been in contact with the Religious Society of Friends for some time I began to recognise names and faces among the cloud of witnesses. They tended to be teachers. In the late 1960's I trained to be a teacher of religion after reading Harold Loukes on religious education:

This is the stuff of the prophets who have rejected
the priests who cry peace when there is no peace

wrote one reviewer of Teenage Religion[10] I had no idea that he was a Friend.

On my first secondary school teaching practice in Sheffield one senior member of staff stayed in my mind because she treated pupils with immense respect and combined unmistakable precision with a great serenity. It was our Friend Irene Gay (d 1995). I did not know that she was a Quaker.

Some years later, and deeply engrossed in ancient Syria, I was struck by the pronouncements of a scholar who treated other people's writings with a degree of tenderness (even when he didn't agree with them) which was not typical of the late nineteenth and early twentieth centuries. Some of the manuscripts and sources concerned were in The Woodbrooke Collection. That meant nothing to me. I had never heard of Woodbrooke. But the scholar concerned was Rendel Harris, authority on ancient Syriac language texts, who became Director of Studies at Woodbrooke. I did not know he was a Friend. I could go on.

Each of these people, as it happens, had taken on teaching roles within the Religious Society of Friends, at

different times in their lives, but to me, who was not a
Friend, their 'secular' work had spoken. I did not know
what had informed it.

***

'How can we best publicise this Society to the general
public?' asked Magnus Ramage in The Friend of
September 27th 1996 ('Ads not Oats?'), wondering why
Quakers lie so low. More than 60% of Friends may have
an answer.

chapter eleven

INDUCTION

I HAVE WRITTEN ABOUT identifying with the group, about knowing family history and about openness with one another. It would be good to hear that many Friends can not understand why I have given so much space to such concerns - for that would indicate that all these things are a reality already for most of us. In this chapter, however, I am returning to something I touched upon in Part One, namely that those who have researched modern Quakerism suggest that when determining if an applicant is suitable for membership, we lack concern about whether s/he has understanding of Friends or not.[1]

In the early 1960's (when I came into membership), people with such limited understanding of the Quaker foundations would have been asked to remain Attenders until they understood us better.

So said one letter-writer to The Friend in some follow-up correspondence I had with him. But

in recent years they have been welcomed as members with open arms,

he observed, and now objections in Preparative and Monthly Meetings that some things were contrary to Friends' ways were being met with 'These things, dear Friends, we do not lay upon you ...'[2] - indicating, therefore, that 'we can do what we like' - or simply with a statement such as 'that's just your opinion, and mine is different'. This is an observation, of course, which matches those of other Friends about the 'secularisation' of our business Meetings.

Jacqui Stewart, in an article entitled 'Friends and Theology' in The Friends' Quarterly,[3] also wrote of a lack of knowledge and commitment to Friends' practice amongst some more recently admitted to the Society. Looking for a way between 'rigid conservatism or total relativism', Jacqui Stewart pointed to the kind of model suggested by Alasdair MacIntyre, in which the internal logic of a thought system is acknowledged and a religion retains its identity through 'tradition based knowledge and values'.[4] But the problem so far as Quakers were concerned was that some had no idea what the 'standards' of Friends had been. Consequently decision-making by communal discernment was not distinguished from 'majority vote' and the decline in financial and practical support of the Society (while Meetings retained their numbers) suggested a tendency to the quietist and inactive.

The outcome might be 'losing the traditional methods by which our religious community finds truth and knowledge', and 'following other religious groups into a wilderness in which all that matters is what each individual wishes and feels'.

Ben Pink Dandelion, Caroline Plüss and Michael Sheeran had made not dissimilar observations[5] and in November 1995, at a modern Manchester Conference of Friends, Jocelyn Burnell spoke of the need for care that openness to ideas, unmatched by in-depth knowledge of our own tradition, did not lead to abandonment of our own identity.[6]

How might such trends be countered? Jacqui Stewart made the following observation in her article:

> We can ensure that those who enlarge our community are helped to become familiar with a lived tradition and inducted into it [emphasis mine].

Induction? Of what kind? And for whom? We should not assume that it is recent newcomers alone who need to learn. It is all of us. But learning can follow only if Friends see the necessity for it. Or to put it in the form of the question which Helen Rowlands posed at the modern Manchester Conference, and which presupposed that as a Society we were not entirely well ... 'Do we really want to be healed?'

Taking by the hand

Induction ('leading in') and also rites of initiation are taken for granted in other religious groups. A discipline is required in such matters, given the assumed sanctity of the Tradition and the care necessary in its transmission. Knowledge of Friends' Testimonies and business methods are perhaps the nearest equivalent for which we might wish to argue. But otherwise, in the absence of a creed or liturgy to transmit, without a history of a formal catechumenate,[7] adult or otherwise, there is a tendency to think that Quakerism is gleaned by observation or absorbed by some system of osmosis. In the days of a majority of 'birthright' members that was probably so. It is not so now. This is why the idea of formal induction should at least be considered.

In some kinds of Orthodox Judaism the concept of community is so integral to identification with the religion that something more than study is required from a convert to it, something more than learning the language of the religion. The proselyte must live in and live with practitioners - sharing the family kitchen where food is prepared; living the routine of the week, the festivals, the rites of passage. Christian churches are closer to us than is Orthodox Judaism and some of them do have formal provision, an adult catechumenate, and ideas less alien to us than we might assume.

On the Way: towards an integrated approach to Christian initiation, published by the General Synod of the Church of England in 1995 is certainly full of weighty subheadings such as 'The Patristic Model' and 'Additional Liturgical Provision' and 'Catechumenal Approaches to the Baptism of Children'. It wasn't intended for the average Anglican in the pew, let alone for Quakers! Yet it shows a genuine wrestling with cultural change and the greater variety of 'inherited traditions which shape expectations'. It speaks of 'taking seriously the starting point of an enquirer' and of learning 'from those whom God is leading to faith'.

It tells of a journey on which the enquirer needs 'the prayer and support of Christians' and it calls on the Church of England to give formal recognition to the status of 'enquirer', as one who, with support, is entering into 'public exploration' of the Christian way.[8]

There is a certain 'Quakerly-ness' in elements of this language. I warmed particularly to two words. They were public and support. They reminded me of how Rex Ambler had described the present Quaker position:

> We have been aware of an increasing variety in the people who attend our Meetings and join our Society. Few of them now come with a background in Christianity, against which they can recognise Quakerism as a radical interpretation. Many come with interests in other religions and spiritualities or in more secular ideas like psychology or politics. This creates a problem of 'induction' for us, but also, at a deeper level, a problem of communication about the truth which we as Friends are committed to [emphasis mine].[9]

142

The problem of communication seems to me to be related to these words public and support.

Induction is a matter of communication. It is gentle rather than oppressive. People are inducted and not (with negative connotations) induced. And this 'leading in' speaks of a taking by the hand, a process of induction and the avoidance of sudden and jarring encounters for which the learner is not yet ready. It requires skill and commitment, love and a desire to share. I have come to think that it is needed, to subvert the danger of Quakerism becoming only the privatised religion of individual interpreters.

I know that my suggestion that we need induction of a more formal kind than we have been used to will not go down well with many Friends. But the evidence of many observers of the Society now suggests to me that we should consider it. Helen Rowlands, writing on 'The Meaning of Membership' in Searching the Depths, reminds us that now 'relatively small numbers of Quakers have a strong sense of involvement in the life of the Society beyond their own local meeting'. This is the privatisation and fragmentation of Quakerism. This is why we need induction. Keith Redfern, writing on 'Quaker Business' in the same volume, told of the secularisation of Friends' business method, and the pluralisation of ways of understanding it. This is a diversification which strikes at the core of our Quaker identity. This is why we need induction.

The seeking and learning process needs to be, in part at least, in the public domain. That is, it should be shared with the Meeting. The Meeting in turn needs to be the means of support. And questions about Truth, as well as about the relation of the individual and the Meeting to the Society's Testimonies deserve to be addressed. Given the setting-in-place of a thoughtful process of induction, the Monthly Meeting could be reassured that Friends seeking membership have indeed had the opportunity of such learning and sharing.

We must not lack the courage of our previous and present convictions as Friends. And we need to learn and teach with tenderness. The teacher is no less vulnerable than the learner. The facilitators of learning and sharing, and that should surely be all of us, may be healing the hurts of some while still remaining wounded themselves. And they are operating in the realm of the partial and the provisional. That comes of being human.

But if there is any agreement worth a mention about what we stand for, then I think we must stand for it. We must ensure that it is understood by those who wish to be part of us and are part of us.[10] This is not credalism. This is taking seriously the validity of our corporate 'leadings' and the experience of our history.

As the end of the millennium approaches...

We need to acknowledge the importance of our ministry of teaching, among ourselves and to the world. It is 'the depth of the teaching' which matters, so that we do not settle for superficiality, lowest common denominators or 'flip-chart' overviews of 'where we all are'. We should not sell our birthright for a mess.

In Part One I quoted from the bard Gwenallt and his declaration of woe that we should know the words without knowing intimately the Word. Those were just the opening words of his poem which in English would be entitled Lost. They went on (using a translation by R Gerallt Jones) as follows:

> And sell our soul for toffee apples and fairground baubles,
> Follow every drumbeat and dance after every flute
> And drown the hymn of Intercession with the jingle of the Absolute.

There must be none of this. We have more than jingles, cheery truisms and half-digested bits of theology-speak ('That of God' or 'a little bit of niceness' in every one) with which to tell of the Absolute. We have never, in the past, been ignorant of intercession, be it prayerful or in the public sphere. We have been capable of practising 'discernment of spirits' and of knowing which flutes to follow. And we will only get into a mess now if we allow ourselves to.

Imagine ...

wrote Ben Pink Dandelion, now Quaker Studies Tutor at Woodbrooke and formerly Resources for Learning co-ordinator,

> ... a Religious Society of Friends in Britain, in which we all truly understand the nature of our calling, and its practical implementation through our ministry as part of the priesthood of all believers.

Imagine ...

> A Religious Society whose history and traditions are all understood. A Religious Society which could be truly reflective, informed, and articulate about its current situation ...

Imagine ...

> A Religious Society which might not have many more answers, but which would at least know the questions...[11]

Just imagine.

chapter twelve

WOODBROOKE, WEAVINGS, WANDERINGS & THE WEB

So I AM SAYING THAT we must not fear to teach or to be taught, and must deepen our contact with the ultimate Teacher. This chapter is mostly about resources for teaching and learning.

We are not short of these, and some Meetings, Monthly Meetings and elders already treat these matters seriously. They are familiar with the books published by the Society to facilitate learning; they share knowledge of non-Quaker publications; they (like many individual Quakers) take to their Friends and enquirers the book which, in their experience, changes lives; they know that different kinds of learning experience are suited to different kinds of people;[1] they keep a library which is updated and which enjoys an annual allowance out of the Meeting's funds; they recognise that paradigms of the faithful and versions of the what and the how of faith, over the 350 years of Friends' existence, may point us to shortcuts on the way, and helpful guideposts, even if we choose to ignore them.

Novel ways of learning and transmitting the Good News of Quakerism have emerged from time to time. The Quaker Tapestry was one such, I think, an act of faith, commitment and corporate activity which has borne fruit in a number of ways (yes, I know it isn't a weaving, but I liked the alliteration in the heading above). And I do not forget that I came to the Society through the outreach activity of a 'Meet the Quakers' exhibition.

In some parts of the Society, however, the provision is less good. Meetings and individuals may find themselves isolated. Some Friends struggle valiantly and in vain to persuade other members of their Meeting to engage in a learning process at all. Over-busy-ness is one reason. Wanting to keep a distance from the group is another, so as to avoid too close an involvement. Feeling no need of such learning may be a cause. Knowledge of one another, vocal ministry, understanding of Quakerism and spiritual nurture may suffer as a result.

'A Wayside Inn'

Of course 'there is no new thing'. Before the turn of the twentieth century it was recognised that an institution was needed to counter lack of knowledge and to provide a space for spiritual nurture. Its work, Friends hoped, would show fruit in better ministry and would meet the social and intellectual challenges of the age.

> We are largely ignorant of our heritage and possess but a feeble intellectual grasp on our spiritual ideals.

as John Wilhelm Rowntree wrote in the early 1900s. And so Woodbrooke was born, waxing lyrical: 'a Wayside Inn ... where the dusty traveller, stepping aside from the thronged highway, shall find refreshment'.[2]

Now, at the turn of the twenty first century, and perhaps to an extent never matched before in our history, we need to provide for our own instruction. For no longer may we assume that every Meeting has a core of Quakers of mature years, with long experience of the Religious Society of Friends and understanding of its ways. Yet as I write (in 1996), Woodbrooke, which serves the Society but is not part of its institutional core, and which for over 90 years has been a heartland of Quaker education, has been financially straitened, has suffered staff redundancies and the need to reappraise its own role. Furthermore the Resources for Learning provision (Quaker Home Service and Woodbrooke), which has produced some of our most-used study material on Quaker identity and other matters, has also been reappraised and its staff has gone.

Staff at Friends House, meanwhile, receive constant requests for information about Friends, whether it be for school projects or for personal enlightenment; while the computer literate are addressing the question of where to place information about Quakers (and what information) on the World Wide Web.[3] We don't only have to address the matter of how the Society corporately is presented, in a world where information technology becomes more sophisticated by the hour. We also have to find ways of engaging our own people and of convincing ourselves of the importance of religious learning and spiritual nurture. Then there is the matter of paying for it.

The worthy issues of peace and social action seem to occupy a higher place in Friends' thinking and giving than does our own spiritual nurture, and provision for teaching about what motivates and guides the work we do. Yet as Pope John Paul II said in an address to priests (I do not regularly quote Pope John Paul II, but we are priests!):

> Beware of spending too much time doing the work of the Lord without spending enough time with the Lord of the work.

Eccentrics and heretics

Who can help us in the tasks of teaching and transmission? Recorded ministers are a thing of the past in Quakerism. Such people were 'recognised' by the Society as gifted and of spiritual depth. Theirs was a vocation requiring 'study, spiritual discipline and a sense of divine call over and above the responsibilities of membership'.[4] Such a thing, John Punshon surmised in 1990, would now be seen as eccentric, 'if not élitist and heretical', for 'there is little place for teaching' and 'there are not many matters on which the Society can speak with one voice'. The separated Friends in Christ, whose Monthly Meeting I visited in the summer of 1996, had as yet not 'recognised' any such minister among themselves.

Yet we have reason for optimism. Despite John Punshon's surmise, we are seeing the beginnings of a more 'specialised', vocational ministry in Britain Yearly Meeting. It is certainly not 'recorded' ministry of the old type, but there are Friends who in this decade have launched, sometimes under Concern and with support, into the waters of the Society, travelling in ministry, looking to advance a better understanding of worship for business Meetings (and the methods they employ), or spiritual autobiography, or ways to spiritual nurture. These are the wanderings in the title of this chapter.

Even learning itself is under consideration. As I write, at the end of 1996, Peggy Heeks has begun a new research project (entitled Making Connections), examining such matters as the provision of learning in the Society, the relation between provision and needs, the gaps to be bridged, the relation between religious learning and spiritual nurture and the kinds of approaches which facilitate learning best.

We should welcome such ministries and hope for more of them. They may help us to cut through the Society's 'culture of silence' which is at odds with honesty, plain speech and sharing, to make room for 'words of power'. And we may learn, corporately, what it is for the Society, too, to function in a ministry of teaching for the world.

chapter thirteen

WRITING OURSELVES

ONE OF THOSE INVOLVED in ministry around BYM was Gil Skidmore. She was promoting a way to expression which may be helpful for those who find speech hard, and who have a desire to do things privately - though the Spiritual Autobiography she was concerned with did not have these things as its primary aim. This short chapter is about such expression.

The Jewish writer Elie Wiesel, in The Testament, penned the words

> My father is not dead. My father is a book, and books do not die.

Like the monastic Rule which, if it were ever lost, could be reconstructed (so monastics are taught) by observing the poor, chaste and obedient life of the best of them, so the Guidance (the book) which formed and informed the life of the one generation shone through to the next. Guiding documents help to transform lives.

Though Quakers have never set final store by any book, both writings and the spoken word of ministry have been very important to us. For some Friends it is the fact of taking spoken ministry very seriously which makes it difficult for them to speak. Once spoken, the words are not to be retracted. So as part of our task of transmitting that of Truth which has been granted us, perhaps some of us should consider becoming a book.

Legacy of a spirit

For centuries Friends kept Journals in which spiritual progress was more important than the worldly events of the day and the round of work. Some of them, like the Journals of George Fox or John Woolman, became classics of Quakerism. But 'ordinary' Friends kept them too. Similarly they wrote spiritual autobiographies, in which the events of life were secondary to what was learned from them. Such things were not peculiar to Quakerism, of course, nor even to Christianity, but the practice has largely died out in most religious groups.

Some Meetings are already familiar with this idea, through Journalling Workshops or in using material such as Writing the Spirit.[1] In privacy and to ourselves, or in a small and supportive group, we too may create something in words which may in time prove a legacy of teaching, of inspiration and of thought-provoking material for others. Alternatively it may be a means to 'clearness' for ourselves.

I think of the Psalmist (Psalm 40:7 onwards) who wrote:

> I said, Lo, I come; in the roll of the book it is written of me; I delight to do thy will. I have told the glad news of deliverance ... lo I have not restrained my lips ... I have not concealed thy steadfast love

and who started the poem with the words:

> I waited patiently for the Lord; he inclined to me and heard my cry. He drew me up from the desolate pit, out of the miry bog, and set my feet upon a rock, making my steps secure. He put a new song in my mouth, a song of praise ...

Here is telling it openly and without reticence. Here is quiet obedience, adversity and depression, joy and a sense of security as well as despair, finding as well as seeking, telling the good news. And it was all written down in that book.

As Rowntree Quaker Fellow in 1994 Gil Skidmore travelled to many Meetings, encouraging Friends to understand and revive spiritual autobiography, speaking and organising workshops on the topic (and not failing to teach, as I discovered when I attended one). Through that ministry and in her writings she has tried to show its value and to explore the many reasons why people may be wary of it. Trust and the 'safe context' for the doing of it are important.[2]

Stock-taking and self-appraisal

Spiritual autobiography is indeed (in management jargon) stock-taking, self-appraisal and looking at mission statements (some only of which may have worked out in practice!). It forces us to confront George Fox's question about our relation to revelation, religion and the past. It provides one traveller's tales through the many years of his or her present.

Encouragement to spiritual autobiography, supported by the Meeting or by a small group within it (if that is what the Friend wants) can help to keep seeking in the public as well as in the private domain, so that the corporate nature of Quakerism is not overlooked. The very process of considering and discussing such a spiritual autobiography may itself be a means to deeper sharing in the Meeting, even if for the time being no such writing (or audio tape? or video recording even? or computer-based record?) emerges. Those concerned may discover a great depth of sharing.

It may be that what some of our autobiographies tell is of brokenness as an unchangeable reality, of lack of rescue from 'the desolate pit', perhaps of turmoil which was followed by peace. They may speak of faithfulness in monotony and a life of duty, and faith which has to reconcile experience of God with the expectation of ongoing suffering. An autobiography need not be a success story in the conventional understanding of such things. Far from it. To show otherwise is an important ministry.

The spiritual autobiography may not even be shared in this present time, if the Friend does not wish it. It is, nevertheless, a form of the ministry of teaching. There are, Jewish precedents too, which have been described as 'eavesdropping on an intimate conversation ... reading a love letter from the beyond' or as the summary of a spirit, which we read with a sense of privilege.[4]

Such writings take courage. But we must not allow the spiritual to be the great unspoken or the great unwritten.[5]

chapter fourteen

CHILDREN

Quaker Home Service produced among its many posters a cartoon which shows a modern-day Friend sitting at the tombstone of George Fox. The 'bubble' over the Friend's head reads something like 'What were young Friends like in your day George?' The answering bubble' out of the tombstone says 'we were the young Friends in my day'.

The first generation of Quakers was young. Many were barely over twenty. Among its earliest ministers were teenagers of both sexes, and some of them did not survive into their early twenties because of the harshness of prison conditions, public response and the trials of seventeenth century travel.[1] We forget this. It was the young who preached Truth and were the channels for it. It was an age of mission.

Our Quaker family contains children and young people. How we relate to them in our Meetings, what we try to transmit to them about faith and the faith is indeed a measure of our values.[2] What we choose to pass on in a Quaker context tells us much about what we believe ourselves to be.

Spiritual Rights

In the seventeenth century no one (so far as I know) wrote about the spiritual rights of the child, but it was taken for granted, in a way that it is not in Europe at the end of the twentieth century, that a child was in need of teaching about things spiritual.

In the report Unfinished Business: children and the churches which was produced by CCBI (and was the product of work done in 1991 by a group which included our Friend Janet Scott) spiritual rights were described as follows:

• A right of the child to the best of the spiritual heritage of the culture in which the child is born.

• A right of the child to express his or her spiritual beliefs in private or in public without discrimination.

• A right of the child to deepen, doubt, alter or be critical of the spiritual commitment in which he/she is born and brought up.

• A right of the child to education, family, and other institutional support complementary to his or her spiritual development.

• A right of the child to protection from spiritual damage and handicap as is reasonable and appropriate.

The right, it said in summary, was to 'spiritual initiation, expression, choice, support and protection in his/her personal growth and becoming'.

Our Ministry of Teaching

Our teaching ministry is to the young people in our Meetings too. I am not one for reticence about teaching. Sue Collins in the useful and thought-provoking booklet Opening Minds: some thoughts on work with children and young people in the Religious Society of Friends[4] asks us at the end 'How can you eradicate the words like "class" and "teacher"?' Frankly this is something I feel no need to do - any more than I want to eradicate 'family' as model. Perhaps this is also because I do not recognise some aspects of the (unacceptable) 'Sunday school model' in her description.[5] But we need to ensure good provision so that good teaching and learning may be furthered. And Friends in many Meetings are very conscious of how hard a task it can be. Sue Collins's booklet will be helpful.

Fortunately we are not on our own so far as ideas and resources are concerned. Quite apart from the fact that Friends speak of reliance on Guidance in all their doings, schools, churches and curriculum devisors have for decades been wrestling with the matter of religious education. It seems pointless for us to try to re-invent the wheel, when so much thinking and research about children's religious understanding and development, the communication of religious ideas, the creation of a good atmosphere for learning and the transmission of values has been done already. Quakers are not so 'different', and their attitude to faith and spiritual nurture so 'other', that insights from other groups would not apply. So I would want to remind us of the great volume and variety of expertise which is available, from Quaker and non Quaker sources, on teaching the young about matters religious, and for spiritual nurture.

However, we need well co-ordinated chains of information about such things, so that those among us who devote time and energy to working with younger Friends can tap into expertise and glean knowledge of publications. We need to know about what materials, Quaker devised and other, are available, about examples of good practice and what has 'worked' in our own Yearly Meeting and in others. For as things stand (and as with adult religious learning), much depends on uncertain liaison at local and regional levels and on the work of dedicated individuals and small groups of enthusiasts.

They need support. Perhaps some feel themselves in need of training and just as we do not have clergy, so too we do not have (as do some Christian groups) full-time diocesan education officers and the like. Under ideal circumstances our Society could provide more material for teaching purposes than it does, of good quality and including audio-visual and disk-based material for use with the young. It could, I am sure, organise courses via QHS, QSRE and Woodbrooke, for those who wanted to learn more formally about what is known of the transmission of religious knowledge, faith and values. Does one tell parables to five year olds? What kinds of 'religious experience' do children and teenagers report? How might mythology be treated, or the Bible? What about God-talk with each age group? and so on.

But such a commitment to the provision of resources for teaching and religious learning demands our money. Would such courses pay their way by being well attended? Are not the small number of staff with a brief for children, young people and resources at Friends House heavily occupied already? Perhaps we should begin by resurrecting the kind of annual Query which was once common in Quakerism. Perhaps Monthly Meetings should ask themselves how Truth has prospered among young Friends in their region in a given year? This might prove a useful memory-jogger, so that we do not avoid addressing systematically questions of the 'what', the 'why' and the 'how' of our transmission of faith and values to the young; and so that we do not overlook those who week by week take on the task with children's classes and young Friends' groups.

Safely secular subjects

If our Quaker family is a narrative institution, are there some stories which we should not fail to share? And why? No longer can we assume that many of the young are schooled in Quaker families with generations of assimilation of Quaker values behind them. So what kind of induction is the Meeting offering?

The matter of 'what' we teach and share with the young is not easy. It becomes less easy if a group is divided within itself and not certain that it can speak with a single voice. I hope, however, that we shall try to steer clear of a particular temptation in a pluralist Society. This is to avoid certain questions and subjects altogether.

Children's classes (or the young Friends' group) have the potential to become a battleground - and that's just for the teachers! Some Friends will recognise what I mean when I write of steering clear of explicitly religious themes, in favour of ethics and philanthropy. Safely secular subjects can become the staples of work with the young, and these leavened with teaching on social justice and caring. The doing side of Quakerism is writ large in what we tell them. The language of being, believing and of the Source which informs and empowers the doing is not.[6]

Such things can prove frustrating for those adults who want the young (especially perhaps their own children) to be fearless and comprehending with the language of religion and of spiritual seeking, and amongst Friends, but who find that it is not being used. Adult fears about (that most heinous of sins for Quakers) 'indoctrination' at worst may lead to the Meetings of the Religious Society of Friends becoming places where hard religious questions are never addressed, where the tools for the job (such as the writings of faith groups) are never handled and where the pronouncement of the American child (which Margaret Hope Bacon reported to me) becomes sadly true: 'Meeting is the place where we don't have to believe anything.'

We should not be leaving our young people bereft of language and ideas which are part of a rich religious and cultural heritage because, for the moment, they may be uncongenial to some of us. Put at its most negative, we must be willing to offer them things which we may have rejected, and which later they may well reject, but reject, one hopes, out of response to the Inward Teacher and not out of ignorance or ill-informed prejudice. I have always thought that the principle of the young being left to 'make up their minds when they're older' is not helpful if we also leave them unaware of the options.

It's like 'Bo Peep theology'. As in other churches some of our young people will go out from the Quaker fold, to return at a later stage. 'Leave them alone and they'll come home' will apply if home really has been a place which is remembered as one of nourishment and honest communication.

'The spark that flies'

We need to be honest. The children in our Meetings may not have the capacity for the linguistic ducking and weaving which modern Friends like to employ, so they deserve our directness. They also tend to prefer the is to the may be; and they may well be intolerant of our haziness. George Fox's 'What canst thou say?' strikes us like a hammer, as it did Margaret Fell, because it has the directness of the unimpressed and impatient adolescent. It is being aware of these very things, of course, which may lead us to avoid the young people's class or the residential weekend, pleading that we are 'not good with children'.

This happens because it is we who can not find the words. It is we (of little faith) who lack the confidence that we can build the kinds of things of which the 1960 Swarthmore lecturer Kenneth Barnes wrote, in a piece now quoted in Learners All: Quaker experiences in education:[7]

> a relationship ... in which the adult and children enjoy each other's company .... free from fear ... a

spark that flies ... flexibility to meet personal
needs, to allow the unexpected to enter ... inventive
and resourceful ... [knowing] all round the subject
matter, ... aware and happy about its uncertainties
and its gaps, its loose ends.

It presupposes, of course, that we are willing to learn
too, to make ourselves vulnerable, and to help others
understand things which may not, any longer, be central
for us. They may prove to be so for them, in time. We
should not close doors against the God of surprises.

***

My first Friends' Meeting was one where there were no
children above toddler age. One Sunday a woman came
late into Meeting with a girl of about seven who clearly
had never been in such a setting before. They sat down
in the front row of a circle, across the room from me.
After some minutes came the stage whisper. 'What
are they doing?' the child asked. The mother replied
inaudibly. There was silence. Then 'Is he invisible?' The
mother assured her it was so. Not long after, the male
clerk of the Meeting rose, several rows behind her, and
read from the Advices in a chocolate brown voice. The
child's face was a wonder. Openmouthed she searched
the ceiling for clues, and then smiled. I smiled too, because
she was not wrong.·It seemed a small parable of faith.

The gift of being there
Just as all of us contribute to the sense and the
communion of a Meeting by being there and in loving
fellowship with the others (even if we do not offer vocal
ministry) so too our young Friends are being educated by
our very presence. The smile and the act of kindness;
the talking with over fruit juice and biscuits after
Meeting; the refusal to treat them, and their concerns,

less than seriously, and as less than the important people that they are, are means to creating that 'family' which we want everyone to feel part of. 'Some Quakers', my son confided en route to a gathering of young Friends at our Meeting House, 'are like your parents.' The woman Friend he dubs 'my favourite Quaker' has no idea why she holds that place in his mind, but evidently she has made him feel good about himself.

Much of the best that happens is mutual learning by old and young, with important questions being asked not during the appointed 45 minutes of 'the class' but in the passing round of drinks, in the planning time for some other activity or in impromptu 'huddles' in garden or corridor. Anne Hosking reminds us in Friends' Quarterly of January 1984 ('A child's gift of worship') that:

> Today children have to bear an unusually heavy burden of knowledge and fear ... they need worship, and all the other aids of religion ... we help them not by our futile attempts to 'keep them in the Society/church' ... but by recognising their own full stature as God's children. If we ... respect their integrity, their capacity to worship and experience God, then they will respect it too. If we share the skills that we are learning, then they will practise them too.

'A child's relationship with God' is valid now.[8] Or as the Advices and Queries (No 19) put it:

> Llawenhewch ym mhresenoldeb plant a bobl ifanc yn eich cwrdd, gan gydnabod doniau sydd ganddynt ...

> Rejoice in the presence of children and young people in your meeting and recognise the gifts they bring ...

Such things take us all beyond 'the children's room', and into the very heart of our Meetings.

Taught or caught?

So what are we trying to do? There is the matter of induction into the Quaker setting in which they find themselves. There is also providing aids to spiritual awareness and nurture.

Can you make people (adult or child) more 'spiritual' or teach spirituality? Teaching about it is possible. So too is the offering and sharing of models, questions, aids to reflection, love-stories to prod its awakening; and

> showing new views, new vistas, to people who had not the foggiest idea that there was a mountain range hiding in the cloud, let alone hills, valleys, plains, jungle ...

as Jill Robson put it in the book Can Spirituality be Taught?[9]

A good environment matters: Meetings and homes in which conversation between creator and creature is acknowledged and promoted, as is the integration of this with the rest of life; places where the God-given potential for full personhood is recognised and encouraged, especially when things look unpromising! If we can give them a sense of worship and of waiting on God as being commonplace, unexotic and as normal and essential as breathing; then at the same time we are opening to them the extraordinary, the possibility of being unconventional and of being teachers and prophets for the future. Meanwhile ...

'We are an army'

Let me tell you about our young Friends' group at Bridgend/Pen y Bont ar Ogwr, in South Wales Monthly Meeting. Ours is a privileged Meeting. It has associated with it a group of twelve young people; with one exception - one five year old - they are between the ages of nine
162

and fourteen. Eight of them, the children of four families, attend very regularly. Consequently we do not suffer the frustration of making preparation for young Friends who do not turn up; we do not have to counter the loneliness of just one, or perhaps two, young people who may prefer to be somewhere else. Many Meetings are not so fortunate.

My teenage chapel group had thought of itself as a gang. That of Gwyn Alf Williams had seen itself in highly politicised terms. Our young Bridgend Friends once (some years ago) congregated on the garden behind the Meeting House with the words 'we are an army'. It helps to have a garden.

Our (converted bungalow) Meeting House is not suited to the presence of a dozen of the lively young. The room for their activities is just a short passageway from the Meeting room. But we manage. We have stopped referring to them as 'the children', and in one respect, at least, our group is different from most in Britain. 50% of the 'core' attend Welsh language schools. For three of them Welsh is their first language. In more ways than one we must be sensitive to the language we use and which we let them use.[10]

My family has been part of this Meeting for six years. My son had to find his place within an already well-established group and some Friends have found the children's presence disruptive at times. It is the parents who take responsibility for organising activities and for oversight of the young people. They are without exception people who are in full-time employment and very busy in other respects. A few other members of the Meeting do join on the rolling programme, but they are exceptional. This pattern does not escape the notice of the young people concerned (who see enough of their parents already, they think!). It is one which many Meetings will recognise.

'Live adventurously ...'

They expect a lot from us. They do not suffer inconsistency gladly, or half-hearted adherence to promises, or adult hesitancy when faced with their ideas. They are a prodding mechanism behind the Advice 'live adventurously', planners and movers, at times dragging the adults along. We underestimate constantly the depth and the shallowness of their understanding and the spirituality which informs them.

We must leave the avenues open, and not block them with our own unknowing, our embarrassment or what we have chosen to leave behind. The young can be very challenging of our 'woolliness' and uncertainty, our vagueness about paths, our caution, our pragmatism. They can spot the flaws and incoherence in the stances we adopt. As they get older it will get more challenging still, we know. They have been good for us parents and for the Meeting, because we have been forced to leaps of faith, enfolded in their enthusiasms.

We know now that we can accommodate a score of 'resident' young Friends at our less-than-perfect Meeting House, even if there is a queue for the toilets in the morning and - given the imperfections of our kitchen - the supper is fish and chips from down the hill (only an adult would have thought that was a disadvantage!). The Meeting could decide on erecting a shed at the lowest level of the garden, as YFHQ, and it could agree that that portion of the garden ('the jungle') should get only such minimal horticultural attention as safety required, because they liked it.

Much-needed domestic improvements have made some difference too (the needs of the young are helping to inform our thinking about the Meeting House). Rewiring has brought extra power points in 'the children's room', and fewer problems when we want to bring in a video-machine and monitor, use a tape-recorder, and so on. We can not compete with the world of technology, but it would be foolish to ignore its many benefits.

Above all we know now from experience that they are capable of devising their own rules when acting as hosts in their Meeting House, and can show great sensitivity to others. Everyone is lovingly accommodating of the five year old - who can keep his end up with no trouble at all - even when they are still an army.

Already we are not enough for them. They know of other Meetings, Link weekends, residential gatherings of Meeting of Friends in Wales. They have plans for a network of young Friends, from all over South Wales at least. Computer literacy and the telephone facilitate organisation. They want a Wales-wide Young Friends' newsletter for their age group, more residential gatherings for fellowship, fun and discussion and worship. They mention worship. Can they get to visit young Friends in America?

Can we meet the challenge? Ours is a small Meeting but one where parents are committed to regular attendance with their children. Quite a lot of what is done is now determined by them, meeting their stated needs and enquiries. It brings us, the 'teacher' Friends, into spheres we might otherwise have wished to avoid. We are having to study, and that has to be good. Also the adults have had to learn to trust each another. We agree that it has brought us together in meaningful ways.

'I have heard you calling ... '

Lest it be thought that Bridgend has devised an enviable system for Sunday classes, it is not so! We know about chaos, hastily-devised programmes, mis-timing and misiudgement and the occasional Sunday when someone will have had to 'take them swimming'. And they know the Meeting's failings.

Here is an extract from an unsolicited poem by the oldest of our young Friends, written after considering the questionnaire which I shall describe below. It speaks clearly of the fact that the older ones among them are feeling the weight of their own maturity. It speaks of the need for all of us in our Meeting to respond by making them feel truly part of the whole:

Should we wait for development
Among young minds?
Or should we act now
And help them interact
With the adults?
The adults.
Those people who go
Into that room
For a whole hour.
And talk about things
Which would never be
Understood by them,
The children.
The children,
So different from
The sincere solemnity
Of the grown-ups.
Two worlds apart.
So unlike,
So near yet so far...

My Meeting has not yet found the answers. Indeed we are constantly discovering the questions. Sometimes I find my Meeting hilarious. It is interesting, then, to know that for some the predominant impression is of 'sincere solemnity'.

Sometimes our young Friends make us sing. I regret having missed the occasion when they were taken to the small Meeting at Trealaw, scene of much Quaker work in the Rhondda.[11] There a Friend spoke with them sensitively and Trealaw Quakers experienced the 'ministry' of a nine year old's conducted choruses of Shalom Haverim ('Peace, Friends') and Father We Adore You, Lay Our Lives Before You, the latter sung in two languages at once. ('Now ... first say the words after me ...') The words of such songs carry the language of conventional religion. I would hate to see them lost from the vocabulary of growing, changing minds, so I teach them songs. I find them a useful starting point for talking about lots of other things:

> Here I am Lord,
> Is it I, Lord?
> I have heard you calling in the night ...

- an introduction to the concept of 'leadings'.

> We are marching in the light of God
> We are living in the love of God
> We are moving in the power of God

- it's a different kind of army. Or

> When the night becomes dark,
> your love, O Lord, is a fire,

- just the thing for epilogue by candlelight before you unroll your sleeping bag in the Meeting House. Or

> And every man 'neath his vine and fig tree
> shall live in peace and unafraid.
> And into ploughshares turn their swords,
> nations shall learn war no more ...

a song made more meaningful by our Meeting House vine, which fills the conservatory and annually is heavy with grapes.[12]

I bring to our mutual teaching and learning my skills as a former teacher of music and of Religious Studies. Other Friends bring their knowledge of the caring professions and of working for social justice, of the Bible, of craftwork, of the Third World and development issues. In Britain Yearly Meeting there are so many Friends with a great deal to offer, if they might be persuaded to offer it.

Traversing great realms

And what do we do? Ours is a 9 to 14 age range. We move from the BBC Blue Peter Well Water appeal to preparing messages for prisoners of conscience and having the chastening experience of seeing one prisoner's reply. The shepherd theme (sheep are a common sight in Wales!), and David's poem (Psalm 23) describing God out of his own experience, are starters to other descriptions, in language and art, of God's character ('goodness' and 'mercy' follow David like sheep). From the making of greetings cards for special birthdays in the Meeting to looking at parables; from the question of what we mean by 'leadings' to life at the outset of Quakerism (some were particularly proud of their cardboard ships bobbing over the painted sea to the New World). And they sing the George Fox song lustily.[13] We used creation as a theme, and for the seventh day had the bread of the Jewish Sabbath which was carried around to share with Friends over coffee:

> Blessed art Thou O Lord our God,
> King of the universe,
> Who bringest forth bread from the earth.

'It's a eucharist' said our oldest and longest-standing Attender, who is also a minister of the United Reformed Church tradition. And of course she was right. It's also a cue for discussion of why Friends don't have spoken blessings and graces. In 1997 we plan to take them to other places of worship, including, we hope, to a Black-led Pentecostalist church.

It is only now that I begin to understand what the early Friends of Truth said about the ministry of children - much of which I had dismissed as typical of the pietistic language of the age. And I wonder whether the 'travelling' of the young from one Meeting to other 'childless' ones might not be a valuable form of ministry - and perhaps an exercise in patience for all.

***

Lest it be thought that these young people are nauseatingly, conventionally, overtly pious, here is an exchange overheard between an eleven year old and a nine year old, in the Autumn of 1996:

Eleven year old (thoughtfully):
    'We are Quakers, and we worship ...

Nine year old:
    'Get a life!'

'More Meetings and a football team':
        the Bridgend questionnaire

We live in trust that our efforts are not entirely in vain. Here is something which has no validity, scientifically-speaking, which is not significant, statistically-speaking, and which has told me some interesting things about my own Meeting.

In September 1996 the eight young people which form the 'core' responded to a questionnaire about Friends, Meetings and themselves. It was anonymous and could be answered in English or in Welsh (some children swapped languages more than once mid-stream). Here are some edited results, quoted with permission and with spelling and punctuation untouched.

Question 'Why do you think people come to Meeting for Worship each Sunday?'

Answers 'For a chance of peece and quiet'/ 'For peace and quiet away from noise and conflict'/ 'Achos maen nhw'n siarad a duw' (because they are speaking with God)/ 'Because Sunday is known as a holy day and is normally the day most other Christians worship'/ 'To pray to god for other people, themselves etc, and to ask forgiveness and guidance in their daily lives'/ 'to pray and sometimes play games'/ 'I ddweud diolch i ddiw ac i ddathlu dydd olaf i dduw gwneud y byd' (to say thank you to God and to celebrate the last day of God's creation).

Question 'Are there things about Quakers you do not understand?'

Answers 4 Yes, 2 No, 2 unanswered. Examples included: 'the stories sometimes'/ 'parents minds'; 'Beth ydy'r wahaniaeth rhwng y cyfarfod yma ac yn Llangranog?' (what's the difference between the Meeting here and in Llangranog? [14]

Question 'What adjectives would you use to describe Bridgend Meeting?'

Answers 'Large'/ 'quiet, weekly' (a wit at work, I think!)/ 'collective, thoughtful, holy'/ 'circled, friendly'/ 'caredig' (kind)/ 'lot o swn' (much noise)

Question 'What adjectives would you use to describe your own Young Friends group?'

Answers 'Llawn o egni' (full of energy)/ 'enerjectic, noisy, friendly, idiotic/ wiled / inventive, discussive, young (the wit again)/ developing, interesting, fun/ doniol iawn (very funny), swnllyd (noisy)/ independent, forward going, rash.

Question 'Do you feel part of the "main" Meeting, as well as of your group?'

Answers 'Na. Oherwydd rydw i yn ifanc' (No, because I am young)/ 'Sometimes ... I think that a few of the grown ups do not take enough notice of the children although some are great fun!'/ 'Yes, I like to take part in the first quarter of meeting and use this time to pray'/ 'Yes because we have a lot of children and other meetings havent'/ 'Yes because I come almost every day'/ 'No'/ 'Ydw rydw i'n teimlo fel un or ...' (Yes, I feel like one of ...)/ 'Yes, I have recently been on the Llangranog weekend and enjoyed it a lot and feel it brought the older kids closer towards the adults'.

Question 'Are there things about Bridgend Meeting you do not like?'

Answers 'Yes. Adults lack of willingness for things'/ 'Nothing'/ 'Weithiau dydyn nhw ddim yn gyfeillgar' (sometimes they are not friendly)/ 'No'/ 'Yes. Parents'/ 'Yes. The adult-child relationship'.

Question 'Do you ever tell other people that you go to a Friends' Meeting or to church?'

Answers Yes (5); No (2) 'Not if I can help it' (1). (This is a marked contrast with the less than 40% of adult Friends who so identify themselves.)

Question 'Has being part of Bridgend Meeting helped you in understanding difficult things such as God, Jesus, justice (fairness), conflict, loving and caring?'

Answers Yes (7) Often (1)

Question What do you think would improve your Meeting for you?'

Answers 'Gwneud yr adeilad ar ardd mwy taclus ac mwy lliwgar' (making the building and garden tidier and more colourful)/ Dubul glazing, more color / 'More meetings with other meetings, soundproofing, newsletters for children'/ 'Split children's class into older and younger'/ 'Topics chosen by children, regular children's meetings'/ (15) 'Canu ... peintio'r shed' (singing ... painting the shed)/ 'Disco lighting ... a football team' (the wit again!)/ 'New library and kid's room. More organisation'/ 'More communication between adults and children. Kids meeting more often. It's too cold. More sanity. Split children's class'/ 'More children'.

They are telling us something: about a rift appearing between the older and some younger members of the group (who are considered less 'sane'), about the effect on them of our imperfect activities room 'double glazing, too cold, sound-proofing', about their desire to meet more often and with others, and about the fact that it is their parents, for the most part, who are the members of the Meeting relating most closely to them. They want a greater sense of belonging to, and being valued by, the whole of the Meeting. They also want to get beyond it.

What can we say?

To be transmitters of tradition, faith and values, to be teachers of any kind, is to be optimists. It presupposes that there is a future and that the transformation of the world and its people will go forward. What do we tell? Always the truth about Truth, always the truths we have found helpful. The young will discover for themselves the truth about us (see Quaker Faith and Practice 23.83).

In Quaker Faith and Practice (23.85) Janet Galbraith is quoted as saying that the two qualities most important to children of today are hope and imagination. 'Hope to believe they can change the world they live in and imagination to find ways to do so'. I would want to add another one. It would be trust, in the movement of the Spirit and in the living God who will empower and guide them in the doing.

That is faith.

chapter 15

THE MINISTRY OF PROPHECY

Prophecy was one of the reasons why I became a Quaker. My interest in it had started with the Bible and the writing prophets of eighth century BCE Israel - Micah, Amos, Isaiah. They had responded to a personal 'call', had experienced transforming 'visions' and had challenged court and people.

In thrall neither to king nor priesthood, they demanded in God's name that religion should not be divorced from morality and should be more than the outward observances of ritual and liturgy. They seemed to pose a political threat. They warned of inevitable consequences if the signs of the times were ignored. They were not so much foretelling the future as 'telling it like it is'.

I knew from teenage years that these were the kind of people for me, despite lurid language in some of the narratives, the strange prophetic acts, heavy with symbolism and the fact that they came of a different time and culture. Our son Nathan was named after one.

'There were in the church
of Antioch... prophets'
(Acts 13:1)

Then there was early Christian prophecy - more widespread and influential than most Christians know. Challenging and encouraging congregations, preaching

173

political dissent and God's vindication of the underdog in apocalyptic terms, deploring the rise of bishops as the wielders of authority so as to marginalise the Spirit-empowered. I researched and wrote about it. Almost every article and book I have written, including this one, has been partly, at least, to do with prophecy.[1]

And finally I encountered Quakerism. There was prophecy again. It was more clearly visible, it seemed to me, than in other manifestations of Christianity which I'd looked at. This was because of Friends' teaching about direct reliance and direct illumination, without need for human intermediaries. It was because of the egalitarianism of Quaker teaching and practice and the acknowledgment (which was true of Jewish and early Christian prophecy too) that both sexes might feel 'led' and should act accordingly. And in studying seventeenth century Quakerism it became obvious to me that the language of biblical prophecy had been central to the thinking and preaching of the Friends of Truth, and in their debates with others. The tracts and letters were steeped in it.

A number of times in his writings George Fox quoted Numbers 11:29 and the cry of Moses 'I would that all the Lord's people were prophets'. In the Epistle from the General Meeting at Skipton in April of 1660 the early Friends, conscious of a great movement for change in the air, had declared 'Arise ... every one to the ministry yourselves for England is a nation of prophets that must spread ...'

'This saith the Lord', declared the women Friends, Margaret Killam and Barbara Patison, in true prophetic fashion, in the Warning from the Lord to the Teachers and People of Plymouth of 1656:

> I have sent my sons and daughters from far
> I have raised up prophets among you ... but some
> of my messengers you have imprisoned and others
> you have evil entreated.

In God's name, then, the early Friends had challenged and preached the demand of God, had spoken of comfort and the possibility of change, just as the prophets of old had done. And throughout the history of our Society corporate and individual acts have brought vilification and imprisonment to those Friends who have performed them That is how it has always been with prophecy:

> I will send you prophets, wise ones and teachers; you will kill some of them, crucify others, and whip others in the synagogues and chase them from town to town
>
> (Matthew 23:34)

or 'a prophet is not without respect, except in his own country ...' (Matthew 13:57); or

> I am driven away like a wolf from the sheep, I am not a wolf. I am word and spirit and power,

as the Montanist prophet Maximilla declared in the closing decades of the second century.[2]

Looking at the prophetic legacy of Quakerism it seemed to me to be as Janet Scott described it in The Friends' Quarterly of October 1982:

> Quakerism is not a spectator sport - it's a vocation.[3]

The prophetic Meeting

I decided that even the Meetings for worship and business were a prophetic forum. For there the individual shared as ministry what had been received directly. Prophets are marginal and troublesome figures precisely because they claim no personal authority but declare themselves to be led to the stance they are adopting - often against their own human judgement. The Friends' Meeting, similarly, is surely a rogue affair - unpredictable, taken by surprise on a regular basis, and not quietly content with a diet of predictable or unchallenging ministry - if it is truly prophetic.

Ministry as prophecy

Paul wrote that love was the gift of the Spirit par excellence (1 Corinthians 13), adding 'and earnestly desire the gifts of the Spirit, especially that you may prophesy' (1 Corinthians 14:1 cf. 1 Thessalonians 5:19). In Quaker terms vocal ministry has served to do precisely those things which the New Testament described as prophecy (especially in 1 Corinthians 12-14). And through such prophecy, faith and values are proclaimed, expounded and challenged. Let me elaborate as to why I think the Quaker understanding of vocal ministry is like the charism of prophecy.

Firstly vocal ministry (in its various forms) is public. By analogy with Paul's argument, then, it (vocal ministry/ prophecy) is to be valued above the private communing with God. The latter may be exhilarating for the individual (and here he had in mind especially 'speaking in tongues', which is a mark of charismatic renewal in many Christian congregations today) but it is less useful in building up others. Vocal ministry (like Paul's prophesying) has a meaning for all who hear it and can be judged. So it is a foil to inward-looking, or purely meditative, or self-indulgent or individualistic practice which is unintelligible or inaccessible to everyone but the practitioner.

Secondly its purpose, wrote Paul, was to edify the listening group (1 Corinthians 14:1-6). Prophecy was a matter of God's offering help, encouragement, consolation, an inspired message or some interpretative teaching. So it is with Friends' vocal ministry.

Thirdly such prophecy/vocal ministry traditionally hasn't been afraid to admonish and challenge (prophecy knows right from wrong); it has not feared the discomforting words of power. For as the very 'prophetic' letter to the Hebrews (4:12) puts it,

> The word of God is alive and active, sharper than any double-edged sword. It cuts all the way through, to where soul and spirit meet, to joints and marrow. It judges the devices and desires of the heart.

It seemed to me that these were things a Friends' Meeting would be about. It seemed to me that Quakers would not be about religion tamed, sanitised, individualised and politically neutral, which is something I am averse to. Surely they would be mediators of the God of surprises and challenges, who puts down the mighty and raises up those of low degree; who transforms meanings. I read about the history of Quakerism, just to be sure, and I found other parallels with prophecy.

Fourthly there was the order and coherence of Quaker practice. The early Friends decided on this, after a period of occasional disorder and incoherent Meetings. This matched the Christian prophetic model too. 'Two or three who are given to prophesy shall speak ... All of you may prophesy, [but] one by one ... God does not want us to be in disorder but in harmony', Paul had written (1 Corinthians 14:29-33).[4] And while the experience of each Friend was to be acknowledged, it was also to be tested against that of the 'gathered' group, against Scripture and the witness of Friends through the generations. Right ordering was at odds with an 'anything goes' mentality. But prophecy was also a means to change and to new insights for different times. As Paul put it,

> Do not restrain the Spirit. Do not despise prophesyings. Put all things to the test; keep what is good ...
>
> (1 Thessalonians 5:19)

and

> The spirits of the prophets are subject to the prophets...
>
> (1 Corinthians 14:32)

In other words, I thought, it would be we as Friends who were responsible, informed by the Spirit of God as the gathered Quaker group believed itself to be, for evaluating, absorbing and challenging what was said and done. I became a Quaker, expecting discipline and that I too would be 'subject to the prophets'.

I remain a Quaker

I remain a Friend certain that the Spirit of prophecy still operates amongst us. I believe that we have a prophetic understanding of religion which deserves to be shared and which is itself a means to transmitting our faith and our values. Part of the key to our daring to be different lies in this, I think. And it is a daring which we must dare to transmit to one another, to enquirers and attenders, to our children and to the world.

The privatisation of religion is destructive of the prophetic function. Unchallenged liberalism is at odds with it, as is ignorance of history and tradition, of patterns and examples. Like Fox's 'What canst thou say?' the prophet's challenge comes of the assumption that things are known, though they may be subject to God-given radical reappraisal, novel reinterpretation or contradiction. Prophecy also works out of a community to a community.

If the Religious Society of Friends sees itself as a people in and through which God speaks and acts, then in its prophetic Meetings it must be prepared to practise discernment of spirits, for not every spirit is of God (1 John 4:1-4). And we must expect the discomforting, the creative, the innovative. These are often the words of power. Lorna Marsden wrote,

The cry of the prophet, comes from those
unfathomable depths within him which direct the
human experience rather than allow it to drift at
the mercy of every changing current of impulse
and nerveless will. The effects of prophecy are
dynamic. It sets in motion a change of heart and
summons to a change of action.[5]

Prophecy requires a great voice,[6] as a Society a united
voice, for there is a lot of background and oppositional
noise to overcome.

Not by committee

Prophecy by committee is dismissed easily as the product
of special interest groups, of political wheeler-dealers or
of naïve do-gooding. Most often it has been the individual
voice, speaking out of experience, pain, and special
insight, which has captured the popular imagination or
stirred others to action. Amongst Friends the voice has
often spoken first in the local Meeting. Next 'under
Concern' it has spread what has been 'given'.

Such prophecy is bottom-up - coming from the grass
roots, rooted firmly in community and conviction, and
fed 'top-down', ie nurtured by the God of Concern. Our
Society functions most purely when we remember the
prophetic model, rather than when we sway to the
rhythms of business management, of decision by
committee or of 'central' initiatives.

In 1995-6, however, I was involved in some 'prophecy
by committee'. There was an ecumenical Christian
initiative in Wales to produce the report Wales: a Moral
Society?[7] This had come of the fact that in 1994 the then
Secretary of State for Wales, John Redwood, had
challenged the churches to play a role in addressing the
state of the nation. Cytûn took the matter on board. This
was a great challenge for ecumenism, for there seemed

to be no guarantee that Christians from a variety of backgrounds would feel able to agree on very much. In fact the opposite was true.

I was one of the steering group which was responsible for (among other things) the 'theological coherence' of the whole. But I was not surprised that, even before it was launched formally at a press conference in the summer of 1996, the report and the work of the specialist working parties which had fed into it, had been dismissed by government MPs as 'Christian communism' from the ill-informed.

The prophet works best as a solitary figure, but as one who incites a following which may provide support. This has been our experience in the Religious Society of Friends. The prophet is a nagging, relentless person, a thorn in the flesh of the authorities, a 'troubler' of people, of kings and of nations, like Elijah (1 Kings 18:17-18). The prophet does not find his or her role comfortable much of the time.

Committees, by contrast, are too comfortable, too unaccountable. Rarely are committees locked up.

Our birthright

On the first page of his 1996 Swarthmore Lecture Jonathan Dale reminded his readers that the churches have survived as one of the places where dreaming is kept alive and that 'their birthright, our birthright, is prophecy and the kingdom'. Without teaching and prophecy, which are channels for discernment of the will of God, we shall know less of what is asked of us as a Society and as individual Friends, for the furtherance of the kingdom.

The cry of the prophet is an important means of recall to faith and values, and an important means of transmission of them. As watchmen (Ezekiel 3:17; 33:5-7) and at the gate (Jeremiah 7:2) the prophets of old saw and commented. We need watchers and gatekeepers, lest we go astray. We also need prophetic visionaries, for 'where there is no vision' the people go astray as well (Proverbs 29:18).

We are heirs of the prophets. As latter-day Friends of (or in the) Truth we are heirs of that promised Spirit which leads into (induction?) all truth, which acts as advocate (paraclete, counsellor), teacher, interpreter and reminder; which does not fear confrontation but challenges us to challenge others to decision-making (John 14: 15-17; 25-26; 15:26-27; 16:7-11). As New Testament scholars have recognised, the paraclete-counsellor-Spirit of John's Gospel is the spirit of prophecy.[8] It is spiritual director, companion, interpreter and moral conscience rolled into one. And it is to be in each of us!

When we open ourselves to it, what ministry there will be![9] What insight about how our past should be interpreted for our present and our future. The result will not be identical with the previous convictions of our forebears, but we will be informed by the Spirit for our age,[10] for the twenty-first century, the fifth century of Quakerism. And that is not the same as the spirit of our age.[11]

Streams and cisterns

Previous Convictions will end with a story from Judaism but first let me recap. Part Two of this book has looked at faith, the faith, the ministries of teaching and of prophecy, and at how we relate to young Friends. It has spoken of the need for us to equip ourselves to transmit what we receive and to open ourselves to be receptors. It has talked about induction, so that we know our family history and are able to make informed judgements about worth and dross, true insight versus mere fashion and political correctness. It has talked about knowing the Lord of the work as a prerequisite for the work of the Lord.

One of the themes of the book has been the relation of our Quaker past to our Quaker present, and the relation of us, as individuals, to both. On these things we build our future. There will be change, but this should not be for change's sake alone, and we may fall foul of deceiving spirits of the age if we neglect questions of conservation. There will be conservation and change.

In the year 70 CE, after a disastrous revolt against Rome, the Jews of Judea saw Jerusalem overcome and the temple destroyed. This was the heart of Judaism broken - sacrificial ritual redundant, priesthood scattered and needed no more. During the siege of the city, so the story goes, a scholar Pharisee by the name of Yohanan ben Zakkai was smuggled out of Jerusalem in a coffin. He was granted the emperor's permission to establish, with a group of his fellow Sages, a religious Academy. Out of it would come guidance for the rebuilding of a shattered people. From such small beginnings there grew Rabbinic Judaism.

Stories were told about ben Zakkai and his circle of disciples. There had fallen on them, and on others like them, the onerous task of making sense and order out of religious, political and social mayhem. Here was a generation which had to meet a shifting understanding of community, tradition and experience.

His immediate disciples are described briefly in the most often studied section of the Mishnah, a portion called Pirqe-Avot or 'The Sayings of the Fathers'. Two of them seem to me to sum up what was happening in those far-away times, as a religion was re-worked for new and challenging circumstances, more radically new and more challenging than the kinds of changes we face. The two were similarly named, Eliezer and Elazar, and they may even have some relevance for us at the end of our present millennium.

'Eliezer ben Hyrcanus', says the Mishnah,[12] 'is a plastered cistern which does not lose a drop'. By contrast Elazer ben Arach is 'a spring flowing with ever-sustained vigour'. Ben Arach was ever fresh, ever innovative, a never-flagging source of God-ordered energy for the new generation. Ben Hyrcanus did not allow the good which had been conserved to seep away, just because the new was coming in. It was precious and had proved life-preserving too. His knowledge and powers of conservation were appreciated. Both men were needed, and they seem to me to represent types in relation to what we receive from the well-spring.

The likes of ben Arach are needed for the vigour with which they sustain the thirsty in the midst - as charismatic interpreters and teachers and prophets. The likes of ben Hyrcanus are needed for the realisation that there is more to a resource than its power to provide instant refreshment as it washes over us. Cisterns need to be well-plastered, lest we lose something vital. In the life-preserving mix are our PREVIOUS CONVICTIONS.

Notes & References

Abbreviations

BQT = British Quaker Theology
FHS = Friends' Historical Society
FQ = Friends' Quarterly
JFHS = Journal of the Friends' Historical Society
JQS = Journal for Quaker Studies
LYM = London Yearly Meeting
MFW = Meeting of Friends in Wales
MQM = Modern Quaker Movement
QFP = Quaker Faith & Practice
QHS = Quaker Home Service
QTS = Quaker Theology Seminar
SA = Sociological Analysis
SL = Swarthmore Lecture

chapter 1 - Openings

1 Gerald Priestland, Something Understood, Arrow Books London 1988, p 247.

2 Keith Redfern, 'Doing our Business', in Harvey Gillman and Alastair Heron (eds), Searching the Depths: essays on being a Quaker today, QHS 1996, p 77.

3 The Siddur is the prayer book which preserves the order for worship.

4 W G Bittle, James Nayler: the Quaker indicted by parliament, Sessions York, 1986.

5 'John ap John and the records of early Friends in Wales', JFHS Suppl 6, 1907.

6 QFP 19.02.

7 See also ch 10 and 12.

8 W R Inge, The Platonic Tradition in English Religious Thought (the Hulsean Lectures, Cambridge 1925), Longmans Green and Co London 1926, p 113.

9 On the lectures themselves Janet Scott, 'The making of an institution: the Swarthmore Lecture 1907-1913', JQS (disk-based) 1/1 1995.

10 Cytûn (a word signifying 'agreement') is the Welsh ecumenical equivalent of Churches Together in England (CTE) and ACTS in Scotland.

11 Martin Davie, A study of the development of British Quaker Theology since 1995 with special reference to Janet Scott's 1980 Swarthmore Lecture ... D Phil, Mansfield College Oxford 1992 (publication forthcoming). From now on abbreviated as BQT.

12 Something Understood, p 247.

13 '... in the middle of the eighteenth century, as many as 90 per cent of Quakers were children of Friends ... In the 1990s a similar percentage of participants have entered the group as adults': Ben Pink Dandelion, A Sociological Analysis of the Theology of Quakers: the Silent Revolution, Edwin Mellen Press Lewiston-Lampeter 1993 (based on PhD research, University of Brighton 1993), p 1. From now on abbreviated as SA. The percentage for those on which he based the research was 84.7 (p 331).

14 For example, the same six letters (BGDCPT) 'soften' and the word for she in both languages sounds like the English 'he' - there's not much to be made of that!

15 Anne Thomas, Only Fellow-Voyagers: creation stories as guides for the journey, SL 1995, pp 96-98.

16 Roger C Wilson, Manchester, Manchester and Manchester Again: from "Sound Doctrine" to "a Free Ministry" - the theological travail of LYM throughout the 19th century, FHS London 1990 (Occasional Series 1). Also 'The Manchester 1895-1995 Conference', FQ April 1996.

17 On the loss of a sense of 'convincement' and a view of the way forward see Alastair Heron, Quakers in Britain 1895-1995: a century of change, Curlew Graphics Kelso, 1995, pp 151-162.

chapter 2 - THE OPENER

1 Arthur J Arberry, The Koran Interpreted, Oxford University Press, 1964.

2 Cf also Job 22:27-8; Psalm 16:11; 23:3; 27:1 and 11; 36:9; 119:105; Hebrews 12:13; 1 John 1:5-7 among many passages.

3 Ben Pink Dandelion, SA ch 1 (note 13 above), p 12.

4 On Arabic language and the Qur'ān's distinctiveness see Sura 12; 13; 16; 20; 26; 39; 41; 42; 43; 46.

5 I know students who can read and recite the language of their Scriptures with great fluency, a language which is not their own, but have only the vaguest idea of what the words may mean.

6 QFP 19.07.

7 See Dandelion, SA, pp 268-9 and the index in that work; also Rex Ambler, The End of Words: issues in contemporary Quaker theology, QHS 1994.

8 David Hill, New Testament Prophecy, Marshall Morgan and Scott London 1979, pp 37-40 and ch 3; Christine Trevett, Montanism, Cambridge University Press 1996, ch 3.1 and ch 4.3.

9 Christine Trevett, Women and Quakerism in the Seventeenth Century, Sessions York 1991; Phyllis Mack, Visionary Women : ecstatic prophecy in 17th century England, University of California Press Berkeley, 1992.

10 Caroline B Plüss, A Sociological Analysis of the Modern Quaker Movement, D Phil, Lincoln College University of Oxford 1995, p 67. From now on abbreviated as MQM.

11 The question was 'Art thou a child of Light and hast walked in the Light?'

12 Book A: 'Our Tradition and Today'. Book B: 'Our Experience and Tomorrow'. They look at many of the things which Previous Convictions touches on.

13 Caroline Plüss, MQM (see note 10 above), p 33.

14 Kathleen M Slack, Constancy and Change in the Society of Friends, SL 1967, pp 41-2.

15 Constancy and Change, p 47.

16 See e.g. Michael Mitlehner, 'The Society of Friends: an experiment in plurality?' FQ October 1987, pp 356-63.

17 Caroline Plüss, MQM, pp 92-3, 96-102. Cf Dandelion SA, pp 289-90 and elsewhere.

18 MQM, p 95, on Dandelion's 1993 thesis p 217.

19 Dandelion, SA p 312. 'Quaker-Christian orthodoxy has been replaced by a pluralism of individual theologies. It is a mythologised view that there is a core set of theological beliefs within British Quakerism' (p 294).

20 Having nothing in common: Elizabeth Duke, 'Towards a vagabond theology', FQ October 1985, 553. The second quotation is Dandelion in 'Measuring Quaker belief or "Do Friends believe?"', FQ July 1991, p 328 (an introduction to his research).

21 SA, p 313.

22 Quaker Song Book, Quaker Fellowship of the Arts/Stainer and Bell London 1981.

23 Dandelion, p 95 cf pp 93, 217 of the 1993 thesis. Portions of SA have the same theme.

24 Plüss, MQM, p 177.

25 Advices and Queries no 5, QFP 1.02.

26 FQ October 1995, pp 372-77.

27 Plüss, MQM, p 99.

28 Jonathan Dale, Beyond the Spirit of the Age, SL 1996, p 50.

chapter 3 - No New Thing

1 Martin Davie, BQT (see ch 1 note 11); Alastair Heron Quakers in Britain (see ch 1 note 17); Caring, Conviction, Commitment: dilemmas of Quaker membership today, QHS-Woodbrooke 1992; The Quakers: yesterday, today and - tomorrow?, Quaker Outreach in Yorkshire York 1992; Now We Are Quakers: the experience and views of new members, Quaker Outreach in Yorkshire York 1994, and other writings.

2 Kathleen Thomas, Quaker Symbols, M Phil dissertation University of Newcastle 1992; 'The Quaker Book of Discipline; a sacred text by committee?' in J Davies and I Woolaston (eds), The Sociology of Sacred Texts, Sheffield Academic Press 1993, pp 127-137; The Sense of the Meeting: an anthropology of vernacular Quakerism, PhD University of Manchester 1994; Carolyn Sansom's PhD study of pastoral care and philosophies of mental health in Quakerism will be presented in 1997, University of Wales Cardiff.

3 Testimony and Tradition: some aspects of Quaker spirituality, SL 1990.

4 Images and Silence, SL 1992, Jonathan Dale, Beyond the Spirit of the Age, 1996, see eg p 49.

5 'Change and decay in all around I see, O thou who changest not, abide with me': Henry Francis Lyte, 'Abide with me', Hymns Ancient & Modern (New Standard), no 13.

6 Edward H Milligan, '"The Ancient Way": the conservative tradition in 19th century British Quakerism', JFHS 57/1, 1994, pp 74-101, here p 79. See also articles in the issue of FQ entitled 'A reasonable Faith', October 1984.

7 Dandelion, SA, p 279.

8 The newly-constituted Friends in Christ (Plain Quakers) as yet number tens rather than hundreds, share spiritual ancestry with 19th-20th century Fritchley separatists (see n 10 below), have begun to publish The Call and to distribute The Conservative Friend, a publication of Ohio Yearly Meeting.

9 C E Fager, 'The patchwork of Quaker theology', A Friendly Letter 28, July 1983, pp 2-3; see too Arthur Roberts, 'Paths towards a

Quaker future', in 'New growth in American Quakerism', FQ October 1986, pp 184-186 and other articles in that issue.

10 On the Fritchley separation see Edward H Milligan, '"The Ancient Way"' (note 6 above); Edward Grubb, Separations, their causes and effects: studies in nineteenth century Quakerism, 1914.

11 Cf too Milligan, 'How we got our Book of Discipline: the revision of 1921 - from doctrine to experience', FQ July 1988.

12 Letter to Thomas Frankland, Selections from the Correspondence of William Hodgson with Memoirs of his Life, Sherman and Co. Philadelphia 1886, p 27. See too W Hodgson, A Brief Account of the Sorrowful Lapse from First Principles in the Religious Society of Friends, John Bellows Gloucester 1862 and also The British Friend 1878, 800.

13 See Heron, Quakers in Britain, pp 114-123.

14 Pen Pictures of LYM 1789-1933 (= notes of Richard Cockin suppl by James Jenkins et al) 2 vols. FHS 1929, vol i, p 27.

15 The best example of such debunking known to me is in one of the DiscWorld novels: Terry Pratchett's Reaper Man, Corgi Books London 1992, pp 9-10.

16 See Alastair Heron, Caring pp 9, 18-24, 32-5: 'Quakers are seen as poor communicators, at a personal face to face level, on matters of faith and experience' (p 32); and the studies of Plüss and Dandelion.

chapter 4 - PREVIOUS CONVICTIONS

1 Gwyn Alf Williams, Fishers of Men, Gomer Press Llandysul 1996, pp 15 and 19.

2 Alison Leonard, Telling Our Stories: wrestling with a fresh language for the spiritual journey, Darton Longman and Todd London 1995, pp 44-6. A turning point for me was a children's story called 'Wandering Horace', which I'd been coaxed into telling as a serial at a Christian summer playscheme. Horace the pig escaped his elderly owner daily. With the prayers of well wishers she got him back. I didn't want to be part of a group which failed to tell the children that people should have joined together and built the old woman a decent pigsty.

3 Heron, Quakers in Britain, p 96; Davie, BQT ch 6; Dandelion (SA, p 315) surmised it might prove to be 'the symbol of the 6th theological age of British Quakerism'.

4 Davie, BQT.

5 Geoffrey Hubbard, Quaker by Convincement, QHS London 1974 (there is a 1992 revised edition).

6 Alun Lewis, 'The Mountain over Aberdare' in R Garlick and R Mathias (eds), Anglo-Welsh Poetry 1480-1980, Poetry Wales Bridgend (Mid Glam) 1984, pp 200-201.
7 But see Harvey Gillman, A Minority of One: a Journey with Friends SL 1988, p 40: 'It was indeed necessary for me to go away so that I could find at a deeper level some of the treasures of the Jewish tradition. The solitude of the search was vital ...'
8 Alastair Heron, Quakers in Britain, p 121.

chapter 5 - The Expedient ...
1 Only around 1-2% of new members in Yorkshire questioned by Alastair Heron had formerly been Baptists: Now We Are Quakers (see ch 3 note 1), pp 11-13. In the pre-publication, pre-full-analysis data for Welsh Friends which I saw, of 173 respondents to the question 10 had been Baptists. More may have been hidden under the general designation 'Christian'. This data does not appear in the published study Mae'r Gân yn y Galon - Quakers in Wales Today, Meeting of Friends in Wales/Gwasg Dinefwr, Llandybie 1997.
2 A L Morton, The World of the Ranters: religious radicalism in the English Revolution, Lawrence and Wishart London 1970.
3 Coming Home: an introduction to the Quakers, QHS 1983, p 3.
4 Advices and Queries number 27 in QFP 1.02.
5 Michael J Sheeran, Beyond Majority Rule: voteless decisions in the Religious Society of Friends, Philadelphia Yearly Meeting 1983, p 87. See too Ben Pink Dandelion, 'Quakers a leaderless group?' FQ July 1991, pp 274-282 and Thomas Kelly, Reality of the Spiritual World and The Gathered Meeting, QHS reprint 1996.
6 Plüss, MQM, p 59; Michael Sheeran Beyond Majority Rule, p 87. See too R Halliday, Mind the Oneness: the foundation of good Quaker business method, QHS 1991. Much of Dandelion's SA reflects this view.
7 Davie, BQT p5.
8 Alastair Heron, Ralph Hetherington, Joseph Pickvance, The State of the Yearly Meeting: where do we seem to be?, Quaker Resources for Learning QHS/Woodbrooke 1994, p 10.
9 Keith Redfern, QHS 1993.
10 There seems to be a consensus about this much at least.
11 SA, p 304.
12 See Dandelion, SA ch 5.
13 The need for such understanding will be a theme of Part II.
14 Plüss, MQM ch 5, pp 126-7.

15 Adrian Cairns, Of One Heart, Diverse Mind: the Quaker Universalist Way, QHS 1994, pp 10-11. See to Cairns, 'Towards a postQuaker Quakerism', FQ October 1996, 83-89.

16 Of One Heart, p 11. Davie (BQT, p 346) from an opposite wing, writes of 'radicals' who 'have tried to develop forms of Quakerism which they think will fit in with the increasingly secularised and pluralist outlook of our day'.

17 ibid

chapter 6 - MANNERS

1 Paul S Minear, The Obedience of Faith, SCM London 1971.

2 David Boulton - see too ch 7 note 6 and 'Friends and the next millennium: the continuing quest for a reasonable faith' in The Manchester 1895-1995 Conference, pp 112-117, and Harvey Gillman's rapidly-produced and impassioned response in that issue ('The vitalising of our meetings for worship'). Also Boulton, 'An open letter to Harvey Gillman' FQ October 1996, 179-82.

3 See also SA pp 141-2.

4 Report of the Book of Discipline Revision Committee, 1994.

5 Dandelion SA, pp 61f. 'The question "Would you describe yourself as a Christian?" drew a 50.7% positive response' (with lots of buts, see too chapters 4 and 6. Chapter 2 of Mae'r Gân yn y Galon, from Meeting of Friends in Wales may shed light on the Welsh situation. Pre-publication data suggests that of 34 Friends who provided additional responses on this question for the survey, 14 declared themselves non-Christian/Universalists/questioners of the use of the word Christian.

6 SA, p 256.

7 The State of the Yearly Meeting (see ch 5 note 8), p 19; see too Ben Pink Dandelion, 'Measuring Quaker belief', FQ July 1991, pp 329-31.

8 Caroline Plüss, MQM, p 63. For a different interpretation of what is happening see Jack H Wallis, Findings: an enquiry into Quaker religious experience, QHS 1993, p 84.

9 Teresa Hobday, 'Faith: universal truth or private possession?' The Friend 1992, pp 1167-8.

10 QFP 11.01 (membership as) 'a discipline within a broadly Christian perspective' and QFP 11.14 (concerning applicants for membership): 'Visitors will need to make it clear that the Society is essentially Christian in its inspiration, although it asks for no specific affirmation of faith and understands Christianity primarily in terms of discipleship'.

11 John MacMurray, *Search for Reality in Religion*, SL 1965, pp 63-4. Kathleen Slack's lecture of 1967 showed that the seeds of change were already in the air. On her farsightedness and the climate of theological change see Alastair Heron, *Quakers in Britain*, pp 77-99.

12 *Advices and Queries* number 7: 'Are you open to new light, from whatever source it may come?' On my previous commitment to ecumenical activity see *Mae'r Gân yn y Galon*, 55-60.

13 John Punshon, *Testimony and Tradition*, p 12.

chapter 7 - LOOSE ENDS

1 John Punshon, *Testimony and Tradition*, p 23.

2 Harvey Gillman, Alastair Heron (eds), QHS 1996.

3 Andrew Greaves, 'To an Unknown God' in *Searching the Depths*.

4 SA p 289.

5 Jean Hardy, 'Why am I a Quaker?', *Searching the Depths*, pp 17-21.

6 David Boulton, 'The Diversity of Truth', *Searching the Depths*, pp 27-33. See too, under the same title, the piece in Rex Ambler (ed), *Truth and Diversity*, Proceedings of QTS 1994/5, Quaker Theology Seminar and Woodbrooke, pp 29-33 and in that volume Rodney Hooper, 'Quakers and the Sea of Faith Network'.

7 In *Searching the Depths*, p 32.

8 W R Inge, see ch 1 note 8. See too Janet Scott, 'Unity and diversity in the Society of Friends', FQ January 1996, pp 25-30: Quakers are 'nested within Christianity ... distinct within it ... cannot be located outside Christianity' (pp 27-8).

9 Rufus Jones, see *Friends Quarterly Examiner* 3 (1869), pp 443-9 and *The Later Periods of Quakerism*.

10 Yes I know that such a canoe would not have vast numbers of people in it. Not only do I think, I do not think clearly. Contrast the canoe analogy in Anne Thomas's 1995 SL *Only Fellow-Voyagers*, p 99. Other more useful comparisons with transport are in Harold Loukes's pamphlet 'Quaker Findings' (Study in Fellowship no 29, 1980 repr) and Alastair Heron, *Quakers in Britain*, pp 150, 123.

11 Alastair Heron, *The Quakers: yesterday, today, and - tomorrow? Quaker Outreach in Yorkshire*, York 1992, p 8.

12 Christine Trevett, 'The women around James Nayler, Quaker: a matter of emphasis', *Religion* 20 (1990), pp 249-273; 'William Erbery and his daughter Dorcas; dissenter and resurrected radical', *Journal of Welsh Religious History* 4 (1996), pp 23-51.

13 In his work The Welsh Curate Erbery had contrasted an understanding of the Church as a 'corporation' with one as a 'free company or society of friends' called and making its choice 'by the inward spirit'.

14 John Punshon, Testimony and Tradition, p 23.

15 Margaret Heathfield, Being Together: our corporate life in the Religious Society of Friends, SL 1994, pp 87-88.

16 Jonathan Dale, Beyond the Spirit of the Age, p 121.

17 SA p 323.

18 Jonathan Sacks, The Persistence of Faith, The Reith Lectures, BBC 1991, p 72.

19 Quakers as 'bridge-people' is a theme of Damaris Parker-Rhodes's autobiographical The Way Out is the Way In, QHS 1985.

chapter 8 - FAITH

1 Modern biblical scholarship suggests that 1 and 2 Timothy and the letter to Titus (the so-called Pastoral epistles) were not from the hand of Paul, despite his being named in them.

2 Martin Davie's thesis looks at 'the core of conviction' and poses six questions (see ch 7 of that work). These are: was the development of liberal Quakerism necessary and was evangelicalism as flawed as it has been portrayed? Is liberal tolerance essential to Quakerism and was the move away from the core of conviction and Quaker tradition justified theologically? What are the criteria for determining which beliefs are compatible with Quakerism and what is the identity of Quakerism? I am not wholly in sympathy with the thesis, but some of these questions are ones we should not be avoiding, I think.

chapter 9 - FAMILY

1 Gerald Priestland Coming Home, QHS 1993.

2 Isaac Pennington The Light Within and Selected Writings, Tract Association of Friends Philadelphia n d, pp 21,25.

3 George Guiver, Faith in Momentum: the distinctiveness of church, SPCK London 1990, p 7.

4 Faith in Momentum, p 8.

5 Rosh ha Shanah = New Year festival.

6 Cf ch 1 note 13. One of the most intriguing statements in SA, however, is on p 102: 'A high percentage of birthright Friends I interviewed claimed a lifelong atheism'. Nowadays the SQIF ('single Quaker in family') poses a special challenge to other Friends in encouraging a high level of commitment, for it may be difficult for the Friend concerned, given loyalty to the 'other' family.

7 Haddon Wilmer, 'Family life - school of faith?' in Hugh S Pyper (ed), The Christian Family: a concept in crisis, Canterbury Press Norwich, 1996, p 135.

8 Alastair Heron, Quakers in Britain, p xii.

9 On the paradox see Yosef Hayim Yerushalmi, Zakkhor, Jewish history and Jewish memory, University of Washington Press Seattle and London, 1982, preface to ch 4; Grace Davie, Religion in Britain since 1945: believing without belonging, Blackwell, London 1994.

10 Harvey Gillman, Spiritual Hospitality: a Quaker understanding of outreach, Pendle Hill Pamphlet No 314, 1994, p 17.

11 Heron, Caring, Conviction, Commitment, p 45, cf too Now We Are Quakers; Plüss, MQM pp 81-2; Dandelion, SA, p 330. Since 1980 membership figures have fluctuated relatively little. Attenders' figures, 1980 and 1992, have increased from 5,880 to 8,995.

12 Janet Scott, 'Telling Stories', FQ April 1991, p 251.

13 Steffan Griffiths, 'Waldo Williams, Welsh poet and Quaker (1904-71)', FQ October 1987, pp 382-388.

14 QFP 19.47.

15 See chapter 7.

16 Christopher Hill, The World Turned Upside Down: radical ideas during the English Revolution, Penguin Harmondsworth 1975; B Reay, The Quakers and the English Revolution, Temple Smith London 1985.

17 Christine Trevett, Women and Quakerism, chs 2 and 3.

18 Jonathan Sacks, The Persistence of Faith, p 44.

19 She also said of Reform Judaism: 'Reform is so much about "feel good" nowadays. I'm trying to introduce them to some legalism.'

20 Harvey Gillman, The Friend April 5th 1996.

21 Margaret Heathfield, Being Together, pp 45-51, 67-75.

22 On 'Listed informal groups' (the more proper title) see Heron, Quakers in Britain, 100-103; Davie, BQT, p 5 and ch 4 on 'special interest groups' as encouragements to diversity.

23 Plüss, MQM, pp 68-9; K H Ives, New Friends Speak, Chicago 1980, p 36: 'I fear that unaggressive personalities may be lost'.

24 Haddon Wilmer, 'Family Life', p 135.

25 Amy Tan, The Joy Luck Club, Minerva London 1990 (ch 'Rose Hsu Jordan, Half and Half').

26 Rita Nakashima Brock, 'Dusting the Bible on the Floor: a hermeneutics of wisdom', in Elisabeth S Fiorenza (ed), Searching the Scriptures: a feminist introduction, SCM London 1993, p 64.

27 Peggy Heeks, 'Disciples or Networkers' in Searching the Depths, pp 42-47; also Reaching to Community, Joseph Rowntree Charitable Trust York 1994. Cf too Edward Hoare 'Can Quaker community be re-established in London Yearly meeting?' in FQ April 1994.
28 Haddon Wilmer, 'Family Life', p 144. Cf too Jonathan Sacks, Faith in the Future, Darton Longman and Todd London 1995, chapter 4.

chapter 10 - TEACHING
1 David Hill, New Testament Prophecy (see ch 2 note 8); Christine Trevett, A Study of Ignatius of Antioch in Syria and Asia, Edwin Mellen Press Lewiston-New York, 1991; 'Prophecy and anti-episcopal activity', Journal of Ecclesiastical History 34 (1983), pp 1-18; 'Charism and office in a changing church', in A Kreider (ed), The Origin and Spread of Christendom in the West, forthcoming 1998.
2 Heron, Now We Are Quakers, p 18.
3 Heron, Caring: 'Are Quakers in Britain approaching another watershed in their history ... Would one outcome be recognition of the greater and ever-growing need for religious adult education ...?' (p 63) ... (and) 'work on the problem of diffidence' (p 60).
4 Heron, Caring, Dandelion, SA, p 289 and elsewhere.
5 On different learning needs and styles see too Yvonne Craig, Learning for Life: a Handbook of Adult Religious Education, Mowbray London 1994.
6 'Quaker adult religious learning in Britain Yearly Meeting', Searching the Depths, pp 88-89.
7 Plüss, MQM, p 63. Cf pp 65-8, including 'no institutionalised system of communication' to novices.
8 See Eric Baggeley's 'Case not proven' (for 'the curse of the cliché' and the need for commitment to study), The Friend April 14th 1995, pp 467-8.
9 Only 40% of those who responded to Dandelion's questionnaire 'mentioned their Quakerism to others "always" or "often"' (p 305).
10 Harold Loukes, Teenage Religion SCM 1961. He wrote the 1969 SL book, The Castle and the Field: an essay in the psychology of religion, George Allen and Unwin London.

chapter 11 - INDUCTION
1 Plüss, MQM, pp 67-8.
2 Introduction to Advices and Queries in QFP 1.01.

3 Jacqui Stewart, 'Friends and Theology', FQ July 1994, pp 112-18, Alastair MacIntyre, Three rival versions of moral enquiry ... (Gifford Lectures University of Edinburgh 1988), Duckworth London 1990. On MacIntyre and tradition-based community see too George Guiver, Faith in Momentum (ch 8 note 3 above).

4 'Friends and Theology', pp 114, 117.

5 e.g. Dandelion, in Searching the Depths: '... a divided culture; a conservative approach to method and a liberal approach to matters of belief ... what is of concern is that we do not fully understand the method': Plüss, MQM, p 67; Sheeran, Beyond Majority Rule: 'Quaker membership comprises participants who are not fully aware of the assumptions on which the Quaker method of discernment of truth is based', pp 84-5.

6 Jocelyn Burnell, 'Following the Light' in 'The Manchester 1895-1995 Conference', FQ April 1996, pp 65-72.

7 The catechumenate was the period when the individual received teaching (catechesis) prior to Christian initiation (baptism). It lasted up to five years. A liturgiologist friend tells me that its introduction in the fourth century was in part due to conversion experiences being a thing of the past.

8 On the Way: towards an integrated approach to Christian initiation, Church House Publishing London 1995, pp 98-9.

9 Rex Ambler, 'A statement of the theme' in Ambler (ed), Truth and Diversity (Proceedings of the QTS 1994/5), QTS and Woodbrooke 1995, p 4.

10 Ben Pink Dandelion writes that he is not calling for 'confirmation classes' (see note 11 below). No more am I. Also Harvey Gillman, who writes: 'How can we do outreach if we haven't the slightest idea of the content of our message?' in 'The Vitalising of our Meetings ...', FQ April 1996, p 122.

11 Ben Pink Dandelion, 'The need for adult religious learning', p 91, and with Janey O'Shea, Making Quaker Disciples: the formation of a people of God, Quaker Resources for Learning, QHS and Woodbrooke 1995. On American recognition of need to learn, and its results, see Sandra Cronk, 'Renewal among unprogrammed Friends in America', FQ October 1986, pp 163-70. QFP 2.82-.82 are useful.

chapter 12 - WOODBROOKE ...
1 See ch 10 note 5.
2 John Wilhelm Rowntree, in 'Present Day Papers' 1899. See Stephen Allott, John Wilhelm Rowntree 1868-1905: the beginnings of modern Quakerism, Sessions York, pp 77-85, esp p 79. See also 'Woodbrooke and Religious Education', FQ April 1983, for observations on teaching, learning and Quaker reticence; Hope Hewison, 'The Way Forward' in A Reasonable Faith, FQ October 1984, pp 397-404.
3 Individual Friends, too, have a personal site on the Web, and proclaim themselves Quaker - that term then being accessible for further information.
4 John Punshon, Testimony and Tradition, p 39.

chapter 13 - WRITING OURSELVES
1 Gillie Bolton, Writing the Spirit: material for spiritual exploration 1994; Writing Yourself: keeping a spiritual portfolio 1995; Sharing Our Journeys ... Journal Writing, Spiritual Friendship and Group Conversations, 1995 (all Resources for Learning, QHS-Woodbrooke). See too Gillie Bolton and Deborah Padfield (eds), Reflections in Writing, Curlew Kelso 1996.
2 Gil Skidmore, Turning Inside Out: an exploration of spiritual autobiography, Sowle Press Reading 1996. Her chapter 'The Past is Another Country' is relevant for some of the topics in Previous Convictions.
3 S Jocelyn Burnell, Broken for Life, SL 1989.
4 Jack Riemer and Nathaniel Stampfer (eds), Ethical Wills: a modern Jewish treasury, Schocken Books New York 1983, xix-xx.
5 See Jack H Wallis (ed), Findings (ch 6 note 8 above).

chapter 14 - CHILDREN
1 See J L Nickalls (ed), Journal of George Fox, Cambridge University Press 1952, on James Parnell, pp 63, 214.
2 Michael Rutter, A Measure of our Values, SL 1983.
3 Unfinished Business: children and the churches (Consultative Group on Ministry among Children), CCBI London, no date but post 1991, p 14.
4 Sue Collins, Opening Minds, QHS 1994.
5 I think it is misleading to write of Sunday schools as places where adults were not required to learn and of worship as something not allowed to children. This is at odds with a lot of Protestant practice, which is the kind I know best. American Friends' First Day Schools also involve adult learning.

6 QFP 2.75 is appropriate to the thinking of this chapter. Dandelion in SA also reported that 'children's classes ... are typically ... on non-religious subject matter' (p 305).

7 Learners All: Quaker experience in education, QHS 1996, p 16.

8 Anne Hosking, 'A child's gift of worship', FQ January 1984, p 228 (and other articles in that issue); 'A child of Light', FQ April 1988, pp 51-6 (and other items in the issue).

9 Jill Robson, David Lonsdale (eds), Can Spirituality be Taught?, ACATE and BBC London (no date c 1987), p 29.

10 The fact that it was perceived as 'English' may help to account for the relative lack of success of Quakerism in Wales. See T Mardy Rees, A History of the Quakers in Wales, Spurrell Carmarthen 1925, eg pp 270-71. See also contributions in Mae'r Gân yn y Galon.

11 Barrie Naylor, Quakers in the Rhondda, Maes yr Hâf Educational Trust 1986.

12 The songs come from many sources: the Iona community, The Quaker Song Book, Junior Praise I and II (Marshall Pickering London 1992) and elsewhere.

13 The Quaker Song Book, No 33.

14 There was all-age worship in a setting (Llangranog's Urdd Gobaith Cymru centre) which Welsh-speaking children would usually associate with school-organised visits.

15 Bridgend young Friends meet fortnightly at present. Members of this group are mentioned in Mae'r Gân yn y Galon, pp 66-71.

chapter 15 - PROPHECY

1 See eg ch 2 notes 8-9; ch 7 note 12; 10 note 1 and note 2 below.

2 Eusebius Church History Bk 5.16.17; Trevett, 'Eschatological timetabling and the Montanist prophet Maximilla', in E A Livingstone (ed), Studia Patristica 31, Peeters Press Leuven 1996, pp 218-224.

3 Janet Scott, 'On being a faithful people', FQ October 1982, p 745.

4 It is this prophetic vision of the congregation that Ellis Pugh reflects in QFP 2.05 (in Welsh and English).

5 Lorna Marsden, 'Prophecy and Mysticism in the Society of Friends', FQ October 1987, p 364.

6 Ancient prophets shouted; eg Luke 1:41; 3:4; Ignatius of Antioch Philadelphians 7 ('I cried out ... with a great voice ... with God's own voice ...').

7 Cymru: Cymdeithas Foesol?/Wales: A Moral Society?, Cytûn/Churches Together in Wales, June 1996.

8 M E Boring, 'The influence of Christian prophecy on the Johannine portrayal of the Paraclete ...', *New Testament Studies* 25 (1978), pp 113-122.

9 'It is profoundly true that God does call his servant unexpectedly in the presence of a congregation and bids him speak unprepared. We may rejoice that Friends have never minimalised that supreme prophetic gift' (John Wilhelm Rowntree, quoted by Allott [see ch 12 note 2], p 75).

10 'A prophet hears not one imperative but two: prescription and compassion, a love of truth and an abiding solidarity with those for whom that truth has become eclipsed. To preserve tradition and at the same time the unity of those addressed by that tradition is the difficult, necessary task of religious leadership in an irreligious age' (Jonathan Sacks, Faith in the Future, p 230).

11 How different is what Elizabeth Barnett describes as the reality of some Meetings (Searching the Depths, p 14): 'We will fill the hour with good and inspiring truisms, so that God cannot take us by surprise'.

12 Mishnah (c 200 CE in date) Pirqe-Avot 2:11-12.